**50% OFF!**

ISEE Upper Level Online Test Prep Course

We consider it an honor and a privilege that you chose our ISEE Upper Level Study Guide. As a way of showing our appreciation and to help us better serve you, we have partnered with Mometrix Test Preparation to offer you 50% off their online ISEE Upper Level Prep Course.

Mometrix has structured their online course to perfectly complement your printed study guide. Many ISEE Upper Level courses are needlessly expensive and don't deliver enough value. With their course, you get access to the best ISEE Upper Level prep material, and you only pay half price.

WHAT'S IN THE ISEE UPPER LEVEL TEST PREP COURSE?

- **ISEE Upper Level Study Guide**: Get access to content that complements your study guide.

- **Progress Tracker**: Their customized course allows you to check off content you have studied or feel confident with.

- **450+ Practice Questions**: With 450+ practice questions and lesson reviews, you can test yourself again and again to build confidence.

- **ISEE Upper Level Flashcards**: Their course includes a flashcard mode consisting of over 350 content cards to help you study.

TO RECEIVE THIS DISCOUNT, VISIT THE WEBSITE AT

link.mometrix.com/isee-upper

USE THE DISCOUNT CODE:
STARTSTUDYING

IF YOU HAVE ANY QUESTIONS OR CONCERNS, PLEASE CONTACT MOMETRIX AT SUPPORT@MOMETRIX.COM

ISEE UPPER LEVEL PREP BOOK:
2 ISEE Practice Tests and Study Guide [2nd Edition]

G. T. McDivitt

Copyright © 2025 by Accepted, Inc.

ISBN-13: 9781637988602

ALL RIGHTS RESERVED. By purchase of this book, you have been licensed one copy for personal use only. No part of this work may be reproduced, redistributed, or used in any form or by any means without prior written permission of the publisher and copyright owner. Accepted, Inc.; Trivium Test Prep; Cirrus Test Prep; and Ascencia Test Prep are all imprints of Trivium Test Prep, LLC.

The Education Records Bureau (ERB) was not involved in the creation or production of this product, is not in any way affiliated with Accepted, Inc., and does not sponsor or endorse this product.

Image(s) used under license from Shutterstock.com

Table of Contents

Introduction iii

ONE: Verbal Reasoning 1
Word Structure 1
Synonyms 3
Sentence Completion 4
Answer Key 7

TWO: Reading Comprehension 9
The Main Idea 10
Supporting Ideas 11
Making Inferences 12
Author's Purpose 13
Text Organization 14
Vocabulary 15
Style 16
Putting It All Together 18
Answer Key 20

THREE: Mathematics 23
Numbers and Operations 24
Algebra 38
Geometry and Measurement 44
Statistics 51
Probability 52
Answer Key 54

FOUR: The Essay 63
Writing a Thesis Statement 63
Structuring the Essay 64
Providing Supporting Evidence 66
Writing Well 67

FIVE: Practice Test One .. 69
Verbal Reasoning 69
Answer Key 74
Quantitative Reasoning 76
Answer Key 82
Reading Comprehension 87
Answer Key 95
Mathematical Achievement 99
Answer Key 105

SIX: Practice Test Two .. 113
Verbal Reasoning 113
Answer Key 118
Quantitative Reasoning 120

Answer Key 127
Reading Comprehension 131
Answer Key 140
Mathematical Achievement.......... 143
Answer Key 149

SEVEN: Appendix..........157

Root Words, Prefixes, and Suffixes 157

Online Resources

Accepted, Inc. includes online resources with the purchase of this study guide to help you fully prepare for your ISEE Upper Level Exam.

REVIEW QUESTIONS

Need more practice? Our review questions use a variety of formats to help you memorize key terms and concepts.

FLASH CARDS

Accepted, Inc.'s flash cards allow you to review important terms easily on your computer or smartphone.

CHEAT SHEETS

Review the core skills you need to master the exam with easy-to-read Cheat Sheets.

FROM STRESS to SUCCESS

Watch "From Stress to Success," a brief but insightful YouTube video that offers the tips, tricks, and secrets experts use to score higher on the exam.

Access these materials at:

acceptedinc.com/isee-ul-online-resources

Introduction

Congratulations on preparing for high school and taking the ISEE! By choosing this book and getting prepared, you're taking an important step in your education and journey to high school.

This guide will provide you with a detailed overview of the Upper Level ISEE so that you know exactly what to expect on test day. We'll take you through all the concepts covered on the exams and give you the opportunity to test your knowledge with practice questions. Even if you're a little nervous about taking a major test, don't worry; we'll make sure you're more than ready!

What is the ISEE?

The Independent School Entrance Exam (ISEE) is one of the most common entrance exams for students seeking admission into independent or private high schools and junior high schools. The ISEE was developed by the Educational Records Bureau (ERB). It is used around the United States to determine a student's skill level and potential in reading, math, and verbal and quantitative reasoning.

There are three levels of the ISEE: Upper Level ISEE, Middle Level ISEE, and Lower Level ISEE.

- ▶ The Upper Level ISEE is administered to students seeking admission to ninth grade or up in a private high school. It has a total of 160 multiple-choice questions, one essay, and takes two hours and forty minutes. Questions are at the eighth-grade level.

- ▶ The Middle Level ISEE is for students seeking admission to seventh or eighth grade. Like the Upper Level ISEE, it also has 160 multiple-choice questions and one essay. Students have two hours and forty minutes to complete this exam.

- ▶ The Lower Level ISEE is slightly different from the other two levels of the exam. It is for students seeking admission to fourth or fifth grade. It contains

127 multiple-choice questions, one essay, and takes two hours and twenty minutes.

What's on the ISEE?

There are five sections on the ISEE: Verbal Reasoning, Quantitative Reasoning, Reading Comprehension, Mathematics Achievement, and an essay. The ISEE tests both reading, language, and mathematical knowledge and also verbal and quantitative reasoning abilities. This means that you will be asked to determine relationships between words, analyze situations to determine if a statement is true or false, figure out associations between numbers, guess the next number in a series, and more.

What's on the Upper Level ISEE?			
SECTION	TOPICS	NUMBER OF QUESTIONS	NUMBER OF MINUTES
Verbal Reasoning	synonyms, single-word response, phrase response	40	20
Quantitative Reasoning	word problems, quantitative comparison problems, estimation, analysis, interpretation of data	37	35
Reading Comprehension	identifying and understanding main idea, supporting details, drawing inferences, vocabulary in context, author's purpose and tone	36 (6 passages)	35
Mathematics Achievement	numbers and operations, algebraic patterns, data analysis, probability, statistics, geometry, measurement	47	40
Essay		1 prompt	30
Total:		**160 multiple choice, 1 essay**	**2 hours and 40 minutes**

The Verbal Reasoning section is twenty minutes long and includes forty questions. This may seem like a short amount of time for so many questions, but you will be able to easily answer many of the questions—synonyms and sentence completion—in only a few seconds. These questions are designed to test your ability to reason and draw inferences using your knowledge of words, vocabulary, and logical relationships.

Like Verbal Reasoning, the Quantitative Reasoning section measures your ability to reason and draw conclusions. Only this time, you'll be looking at numbers and quantities instead of words and phrases. Questions might ask you about numbers in a series, or to compare numeric or geometric quantities (comparing shapes). Use of a calculator is prohibited. You'll have thirty-five minutes to answer thirty-seven questions.

The Reading Comprehension section is just that: reading. You will have thirty-five minutes to read six passages with about five questions each, for a total of thirty-six questions. Passages will be both informational and literary (fiction). Questions will test your comprehension skills by asking you to determine the main idea and supporting details of the passage, to draw inferences about the passage, to understand the author's tone and message, or to recall information about the characters, the organization of the passage, or specific vocabulary words that appear in the passage.

On the Mathematics Achievement section, questions address numbers and operations, including fractions, decimals, and percentages; geometry; algebraic thinking; data analysis; and units and measurement. Expect to solve equations, choose true statements, find area and perimeter, and determine measurements. You will have forty minutes to answer forty-seven questions. As on Quantitative Reasoning, no calculators are allowed.

Finally, the Essay section tests your knowledge of grammar, usage, and your ability to express yourself in a clear and organized manner in Standard English. You will be asked about an interesting topic. The essay is your chance to tell the school more about yourself. You do not need to use any outside information; just your own thoughts and ideas. While writing, be aware of punctuation, capitalization, spelling, and grammar. Take time to organize your ideas and use examples and expressive language. On all levels of the ISEE, students will have thirty minutes to write the essay.

How is the ISEE Scored?

You cannot pass or fail the ISEE. You will receive an Individual Score Report (ISR) a few days after the exam. You will receive a raw score, which is simply the number of questions you answered correctly. This score is converted into a scaled score, which will be a number from 760 – 940. The more questions you answered correctly, the closer your score will be to 940.

On the ISEE, no points are deducted for incorrect answers, so you should always guess even if you don't know the answer to a question: you may get it right!

HELPFUL HINT:
Remember, scores and percentile rankings are just a few tools schools use to determine admission. It is important to do as well as you can, and this book is designed to support you. Even if you are stronger in some subjects than others, the scoring on the ISEE will help schools understand your strengths.

You will also receive a stanine score. A stanine score is based on percentile ranks. Stanine scores range from 1 – 9. A stanine score of 1 – 3 is below average, from 4 – 6 is average, and from 7 – 9 is above average.

How is the ISEE Administered?

The ISEE is administered throughout the year. Check online at www.iseetest.org to find a school or test center offering the exam near you. After you register, you will receive an email confirmation of registration.

If you need an accommodation for the ISEE, such as extra time, you must submit supporting documentation.

Only No. 2 pencils and pens with blue or black ink are allowed in the exam room. Students may not bring any scratch paper, electronic devices, cell phones, dictionaries, calculators, or calculator watches into the exam room. Students will receive a five-minute break after the Quantitative Reasoning section and another five-minute break after the Mathematics Achievement section.

About This Guide

This guide will help you to master the most important test topics and develop critical test-taking skills. We have built features into our books to prepare you for your tests and increase your score. Along with a detailed summary of the format, content, and scoring of the ISEE, we offer in-depth overviews of the content knowledge required to pass the exams. In the review you'll find sidebars that provide interesting information, highlight key concepts, and review content so that you can solidify your understanding of each exam's concepts. You can also test your knowledge with sample questions throughout the text and practice questions that reflect the content and format of the exams. We're pleased you've chosen Accepted, Inc. to be a part of your educational journey!

CHAPTER ONE
Verbal Reasoning

The ISEE **VERBAL REASONING** section includes two types of questions: synonyms and sentence completions. The questions will test your vocabulary and your ability to use context clues in a sentence.

Word Structure

Vocabulary is a big part of many high school entrance exams, but you don't have to memorize long lists of words to do well. Instead, you can use word structure to figure out the definition of words.

Many words can be broken down into three main parts to help determine their meaning:

> **PREFIX — ROOT — SUFFIX**

PREFIXES are elements added to the beginning of a word, and **SUFFIXES** are elements added to the end of the word; together they are known as **AFFIXES**. They carry assigned meanings and can be attached to a word to completely change the word's meaning or to enhance the word's original meaning.

Let's use the word *"prefix"* itself as an example: *"fix"* means to place something securely, and *pre–* means before. Therefore, *"prefix"* means to place something before or in front of.

Now let's look at a suffix: in the word *"fearful,"* *"fear"* is the root word. The suffix *–ful* means full of. Thus, *"fearful"* means being full of fear or being afraid.

The **ROOT** is what is left when you take away the prefixes and suffixes from a word. For example, in the word *"unclear,"* if you take away the prefix *un–*, you have the root *"clear."*

Roots are not always recognizable words because they often come from Latin or Greek words, such as *nat*, a Latin root meaning born. The word "*native*," which means a person born in a referenced place, comes from this root.

The table below shows some common affixes and root words. (A more thorough list with detailed examples is in the appendix.)

TABLE 1.1. Common Affixes and Root Words		
Prefixes	**Root Words**	**Suffixes**
a–, an–, im–, in–, un– (without, not) ab– (away from) ante– (before) anti– (against) bi–, di– (two) dis– (not, apart) ex– (out) micro– (small) omni– (all) over– (excessively) pre– (before) re– (again) sym– (with) uni– (single)	ambi (both) aud (to hear) bell (combative) bene (good) contra (against) dys (bad, impaired) equ (equal) morph (shape)	–able, –ible (capable) –dom (quality) –en (made of) –ful (full of) –ian (related to) –ine (nature of) –ment (act of)

EXAMPLES

Select the answer that most closely matches the definition of the given word.

1. BELLICOSE
    - **A)** misbehaved
    - **B)** friendly
    - **C)** scared
    - **D)** aggressive

2. REJUVENATED
    - **A)** established
    - **B)** invigorated
    - **C)** improved
    - **D)** motivated

3. CIRCUMSPECT
    - **A)** round
    - **B)** guarded
    - **C)** dominant
    - **D)** winding

4. CONCURRENT
    A) surging
    B) splashy
    C) sophisticated
    D) simultaneous

5. PATRIARCH
    A) patriotic person
    B) wise counselor
    C) male leader
    D) mother figure

Synonyms

When different words mean the same thing, they are **SYNONYMS**. For the ISEE synonym questions, you will be given a word and then asked to choose a word that has the same meaning.

VERBAL SKILLS (SYNONYMS) QUESTION FORMAT

MICROSCOPIC
    A) tiny
    B) unusual
    C) enormous
    D) hungry

Choice A is the correct answer. To answer this question, study the given word. The prefix *micro–* means "small." The word *tiny* also means "small," meaning it is a synonym for "microscopic."

Having a large vocabulary will obviously help with these questions, but you can also use root words and affixes to determine the meaning of unfamiliar words. Check the prefixes: does the prefix on the word correspond to the meaning of any of the answer choices? If so, you have a hint that the words might have a related meaning.

If you can't figure out the exact meaning of the word, try to figure out its tone. Does it have a positive or negative prefix? Is it a word you've seen in a positive or negative context before? Then, try to choose a word that matches the tone of the word in the question.

TEACHING TIPS:
Help students develop their understanding of synonyms by having them make lists of synonyms for common words (either out loud or on paper). You can turn it into a game by seeing who can list the most synonyms for a particular word.

CONTINUE ⟶

EXAMPLES

6. ADVANCE
   A) promote
   B) abduct
   C) destroy
   D) review

7. RUDIMENTARY
   A) impolite
   B) basic
   C) juvenile
   D) innovative

8. IMPARTIAL
   A) fond
   B) incomplete
   C) objective
   D) mathematical

9. PRUDENT
   A) sensible
   B) inquisitive
   C) terrified
   D) modest

10. ACRIMONIOUS
    A) bitter
    B) inedible
    C) rotten
    D) loud

Sentence Completion

Sentence completion questions will give you a sentence with one or two words missing. You will need to choose the word(s) that best complete the sentence.

VERBAL REASONING (SENTENCE COMPLETION) QUESTION FORMAT

Once Jaelyn learned the code, she was able to _____ its meaning.

A) endure
B) modify
C) misunderstand
D) decipher

Choice D is the correct answer. To answer the question, think about the context of the sentence. Once Jaelyn has learned the code, she will understand its meaning. So, we need a word that means "to understand."

Using your knowledge of roots and prefixes, you can figure out what "decipher" means: the prefix *de–* means "to undo." The root word *cipher* means "secret" or "code." Thus the word *decipher* means "to understand" or "to figure out."

CONTEXT CLUES can be used to solve sentence completion questions. To use context clues, look for words in the sentence that tell you what kind of word will go in the blank.

RESTATEMENT CLUES state the definition of a word in the sentence. The definition is often set apart from the rest of the sentence by a comma, parentheses, or a colon. This structure is common in sentence completion questions.

> Teachers should understand the basics of cognition, how students apply new information to other settings.
>
> The meaning of "cognition" is restated following the comma as the ability to "apply new information to other settings." In sentence completion questions, look for parts of the sentence that might restate the meaning of the missing word.

TEACHING TIPS: Encourage your student to explain why they chose a particular answer choice as you complete practice items. This will enable you to correct misconceptions and also to understand the connections the student is making.

CONTRAST CLUES include the opposite meaning of a word. Words like "but," "on the other hand," and "however" are tip-offs that a sentence contains a contrast clue.

> The teacher offered remedial materials to the struggling student, but the student wanted to read more advanced books.
>
> "Remedial" is contrasted with "more advanced," so the definition of "remedial" is "basic" or "general."

POSITIVE/NEGATIVE CLUES tell you whether a word has a positive or negative meaning.

> The teaching assistant suggested offering enrichment to the student who had quickly mastered the required curriculum.
>
> The positive descriptions "quickly" and "mastered" suggest that "enrichment" has a positive meaning.

EXAMPLES

11. The dog was _____ in the face of danger, braving the fire to save the girl trapped inside the building.
    - A) overwhelmed
    - B) dauntless
    - C) imaginative
    - D) startled

12. Beth did not spend any time preparing for the test, but Tyrone kept a _____ study schedule.
    - A) rigorous
    - B) unprecedented
    - C) analytical
    - D) strange

13. Because she was an _____ runner, Georgette was a _____ opponent on the racetrack.
    - A) avid...formidable
    - B) exotic...challenging
    - C) accomplished...weak
    - D) ungainly...gullible

14. The editor preferred a _____ writing style, so he cut 500 words from the article.
    - A) descriptive
    - B) graceful
    - C) friendly
    - D) terse

15. Michael's upbeat personality _____ the tension in the room, and the party continued happily.
    - A) created
    - B) diminished
    - C) elided
    - D) exaggerated

Answer Key

1. **D) is correct.** The prefix *belli–* means "combative" or "warlike." The word choice closest in meaning to combative is "aggressive."

2. **B) is correct.** The root word *juven* means "young" and the prefix *re–* means "again," so *rejuvenate* means "to be made young again."

3. **B) is correct.** The root word *circum* means "around," and the root word *specere* means "to look," so a *circumspect* person looks cautiously around herself and is guarded.

4. **D) is correct.** The prefix *con–* means "with or together," and the root word *concurrere* means "to run together." Two or more *concurrent* events happen at the same time, or simultaneously.

5. **C) is correct.** The root word *pater* means "father," and the root word *arkhein* means "to rule," so a patriarch is a man who leads his family.

6. **A) is correct.** "Advance" and "promote" both mean "to move something or someone forward." Note the prefix *ad–* in "advance." The prefix *ad–* means "toward." Likewise, the prefix *pro–* in "promote" means forward. That's a clue that the words are related. To advance something is to promote it, to push it forward.

7. **B) is correct.** *Rudimentary* means "basic or elementary." For example, familiarity with the alphabet is a rudimentary reading skill that children learn at a young age.

8. **C) is correct.** The prefix *im–* means "not," and the root word *partial* means "biased," so an impartial jury is one whose members are not biased and are therefore able to evaluate evidence in an objective, unprejudiced manner.

9. **A) is correct.** *Prudent* means "wise or judicious." For example, a prudent decision is a wise, practical one.

10. **A) is correct.** The root word *acri* in *acrid*, *acrimony*, and *acrimonious* means "sharp and sour," and the suffix *–ous* means "possessing or full of." So, an acrimonious relationship is full of bitterness.

11. **B) is correct.** Demonstrating bravery in the face of danger would be *fearless*. The restatement clue (braving) tells you exactly what the word means.

12. **A) is correct.** The word *"but"* tells us that Tyrone studied in a different way from Beth, which means it is a contrast clue. If Beth did not study hard, then Tyrone did. The best answer, therefore, is Choice A, *rigorous*.

Verbal Reasoning

13. **A) is correct.** The word "because" suggests the two words in the blanks have a cause-and-effect relationship. Only Choice A fits. *Avid* means "enthusiastic," and *formidable* means "impressive." An avid runner is likely to be a formidable opponent in a race—an impressive runner, difficult to beat.

14. **D) is correct.** The clue here is "cut 500 words." *Terse* means "few words," so if the editor preferred a terse writing style, he would cut words from the article.

15. **B) is correct.** The sentence contains several positive clues ("upbeat," "happily"). The only answer choice that creates a positive sentence is *diminished*, which means to "to make less."

CHAPTER TWO
Reading Comprehension

On the ISEE reading comprehension section, you will be asked to read a short passage and then answer questions about it. There will be six passages, each of which will be around 350 words. The questions will address six general topics:

1. **MAIN IDEA:** what is the overall message of the passage?
2. **SUPPORTING IDEAS:** how does the passage support the main idea?
3. **INFERENCES:** what conclusions can you draw from the passage?
4. **ORGANIZATION:** how is the passage organized?
5. **VOCABULARY:** what do words in the passage mean?
6. **TONE AND STYLE:** how does the writer use language?

READING COMPREHENSION QUESTION FORMAT

It is negligence for an adult to be unable to swim. A person who can't swim is a danger to himself and to others. Every man, woman, and child should learn. Children as young as four can learn: no one is too young, and no one is too old. If you haven't learned yet, there is still time.

The primary purpose of the passage is to

- **A)** encourage the reader to learn to swim.
- **B)** explain how people who cannot swim are a danger to others.
- **C)** inform the reader that swimming is easy.
- **D)** argue that people who cannot swim should be punished.

Choice A is correct. The author argues that "every man, woman, and child should learn" to swim and addresses the reader directly by saying "there is still time" for them to learn to swim.

The Main Idea

The **MAIN IDEA** of a text is the argument the author is trying to make about a particular **TOPIC**. Every sentence in a passage should support or address the main idea in some way.

The main idea is the author making an argument, just like you might do in conversation. Imagine you are hungry for dinner, and you want pizza. You need to talk to your family and convince them to eat pizza for dinner. The **TOPIC** of your conversation is dinner, and the **MAIN IDEA** is that the family should eat pizza for dinner.

Let's look at an example passage to see how to identify the topic and main idea.

> Babe Didrikson Zaharias, one of the most decorated female athletes of the twentieth century, is an inspiration for everyone. Born in 1911 in Beaumont, Texas, Zaharias lived in a time when women were considered second class to men, but she never let that stop her from becoming a champion. Zaharias was one of seven children in a poor immigrant family and was competitive from an early age. As a child she excelled at most things she tried, especially sports, which continued into high school and beyond. After high school, Zaharias played amateur basketball for two years and soon after began training in track and field. Zaharias represented the United States in the 1932 Los Angeles Olympics. Even though women were only allowed to enter three events, she won two gold medals and one silver in track and field events.

The topic of this paragraph is obviously Babe Zaharias—the whole passage describes events from her life. To figure out the main idea, consider what the writer is saying about Zaharias. The passage describes her life but focuses mostly on her accomplishments and the difficulties she overcame. The writer is saying that Zaharias is someone who should be admired for her determination and skill. That is the main idea and what unites all the information in the paragraph.

The topic, and sometimes the main idea of a paragraph, is introduced in the **TOPIC SENTENCE**. The topic sentence usually appears early in a passage. The first sentence in the example paragraph above about Babe Zaharias states the topic and main idea: *"Babe Didrikson Zaharias, one of the most decorated female athletes of the twentieth century, is an inspiration for everyone."*

There may also be a **SUMMARY SENTENCE** at the end of a passage. As its name suggests, this sentence sums up the passage, often by restating the main idea and the author's key evidence supporting it.

> **EXAMPLE**
> From far away it's easy to imagine the surface of our solar system's planets as enigmas—how could we ever know what those far-flung planets really look like? It turns out, however, that scientists have a number of tools that allow them to examine many planets' surfaces. The topography of Venus, for

example, has been explored by several space probes, including the Russian Venera landers and NASA's Magellan orbiter.

In addition to these long-range probes, NASA has also used its series of "great observatories" to study distant planets. These four massively powerful orbiting telescopes are the famous Hubble Space Telescope, the Compton Gamma Ray Observatory, the Chandra X-Ray Observatory, and the Spitzer Space Telescope.

Such powerful telescopes aren't just found in space: NASA uses Earth-based telescopes as well. Scientists at the National Radio Astronomy Observatory in Charlottesville, Virginia, have spent decades using radio imaging to build an incredibly detailed portrait of Venus's surface.

1. Which of the following sentences best describes the main idea of the passage?
   A) It's impossible to know what the surfaces of other planets are really like.
   B) Telescopes are an important tool for scientists studying planets in our solar system.
   C) Venus's surface has many of the same features as Earth's.
   D) Scientists use a variety of advanced technologies to study the surfaces of other planets.

Supporting Ideas

SUPPORTING IDEAS reinforce the author's main idea. Let's go back to the conversation about what to eat for dinner. If you want to convince your family to order pizza, you might present a number of supporting ideas: there's no need to cook, it's easy to clean up, and so on. The authors of the reading comprehension passages will similarly present ideas that support their main idea.

Let's look again at the passage about athlete Babe Zaharias.

> Babe Didrikson Zaharias, one of the most decorated female athletes of the twentieth century, is an inspiration for everyone. Born in 1911 in Beaumont, Texas, Zaharias lived in a time when women were considered second class to men, but she never let that stop her from becoming a champion. Babe was one of seven children in a poor immigrant family and was competitive from an early age. As a child she excelled at most things she tried, especially sports, which continued into high school and beyond. After high school, Babe played amateur basketball for two years and soon after began training in track and field. Zaharias represented the United States in the 1932 Los Angeles Olympics. Even though women were only allowed to enter three events, she won two gold medals and one silver in track and field events.

Remember that the main idea of the passage is that Zaharias is someone to admire—an idea introduced in the opening sentence. The remainder of the paragraph provides ideas or details that support this assertion. These details include the circumstances of her childhood, her childhood success at sports, and the medals she won at the Olympics.

When looking for supporting ideas, be alert for **SIGNAL WORDS**. These signal words tell you that the author is about to introduce a supporting idea. Common signal words include:

- for example
- specifically
- in addition
- furthermore
- for instance
- others
- in particular
- some

EXAMPLE

Exercise is critical for healthy development in children. Today in the United States, there is an epidemic of poor childhood health; many of these children will face further illnesses in adulthood that are due to poor diet and lack of exercise now. This is a problem for all Americans, especially with the rising cost of health care.

It is vital that school systems and parents encourage children to engage in a minimum of thirty minutes of cardiovascular exercise each day, mildly increasing their heart rate for a sustained period. This is proven to decrease the likelihood of developmental diabetes, obesity, and a multitude of other health problems. Also, children need a proper diet, rich in fruits and vegetables, so they can develop physically and learn healthy eating habits early on.

2. The author states that many adulthood illnesses are the result of
   A) a diet rich in fruits and vegetables.
   B) poor diet and lack of exercise in childhood.
   C) excessive cardiovascular exercise during childhood.
   D) children not being taken to the doctor.

TIPS FOR PARENTS:
Make sure your student understands that just because an answer choice is true doesn't make it the correct answer. The correct answer needs to come from the passage, not from their own experience.

Making Inferences

In addition to understanding the main idea and factual content of a passage, you will also be asked to make inferences about the passage. An **INFERENCE** is a conclusion that is not directly stated in the passage but is based on information found there. In an excerpt from a fictional work, for example, you might be asked to anticipate what the character would do next. In a nonfiction passage, you might be asked which statement the author of the passage would agree with.

To answer such questions, you need a solid understanding of the topic and main idea of the passage. Armed with this information, you can figure out which of the answer choices best fits the criteria (or, alternatively, which do not). For example, if the author of the passage is advocating for safer working conditions in factories, any details that could be added to the passage should support that idea. You might add sentences that contain information about the number of accidents that occur in factories or that outline a new plan for fire safety.

> **TEACHING TIPS:**
> You can use short videos, TV episodes, or movies to help students make inferences. For example, after a TV episode ends, ask your student what they think the characters will do next. What did they see on TV that led to their answer?

EXAMPLE

Alfie closed his eyes and took several deep breaths. He was trying to ignore the sounds of the crowd, but even he had to admit that it was hard not to notice the tension in the stadium. He could feel 50,000 sets of eyes burning through his skin—this crowd expected perfection from him. He took another breath and opened his eyes, setting his sights on the soccer ball resting peacefully in the grass. One shot, just one last shot, between his team and the championship. He didn't look up at the goalie, who was jumping nervously on the goal line just a few yards away. Afterward, he would swear he didn't remember anything between the referee's whistle and the thunderous roar of the crowd.

3. Which of the following conclusions is best supported by the passage?
   A) Alfie passed out on the field and was unable to take the shot.
   B) The goalie blocked Alfie's shot.
   C) Alfie scored the goal and won his team the championship.
   D) The referee declared the game a tie.

Author's Purpose

Authors typically write with a purpose. Sometimes referred to as "intention," an author's purpose lets us know why the author is writing and what he or she would like to accomplish. There are many reasons an author might write, but these reasons generally fall into four categories: narrative, persuasive, informational, or instructive.

- **NARRATIVE** writing tells a story to entertain. The writing may include vivid characters, exciting plot twists, or beautiful, figurative language.
- **PERSUASIVE** writing attempts to persuade the reader to accept an idea. The passage may present an argument or contain convincing examples that support the author's point of view.

> **TEACHING TIPS:**
> Ask your student to come up with real life examples of narrative, persuasive, informational, and instructional writing. Then ask them to describe how they decided what category the writing belonged in.

- **INFORMATIONAL** writing describes something, such as a person, place, thing, or event. It is characterized by detailed descriptions and a lack of persuasive elements (meaning it is written to inform the reader, not persuade them).
- **INSTRUCTIONAL** writing explains a process or procedure. It may include step-by-step instructions or present information in a sequence.

EXAMPLE

One of my summer reading books was *Mockingjay*. I was captivated by the adventures of the main character and the complicated plot of the book. However, I would argue that the ending didn't reflect the excitement of the story. Given what a powerful personality the main character has, I felt like the ending didn't do her justice.

4. Which of the following best captures the author's purpose?
   A) explain the plot of the novel *Mockingjay*
   B) persuade the reader that the ending of *Mockingjay* is inferior
   C) list the novels she read during the summer
   D) explain why the ending of a novel is important

Text Organization

Authors can organize their writing in many different ways. These distinct organizational patterns, referred to as **TEXT STRUCTURE**, use the logical relationships between ideas to improve the readability and coherence of a text. The most common ways passages are organized include:

- **PROBLEM-SOLUTION**: the author outlines a problem and then discusses a solution.
- **COMPARISON-CONTRAST**: the author presents two situations and then discusses the similarities and differences.
- **CAUSE-EFFECT**: the author recounts an action and then discusses the resulting effects.
- **DESCRIPTIVE**: the author describes an idea, object, person, or other item in detail.

EXAMPLE

The issue of public transportation has begun to haunt the fast-growing cities of the southern United States. Unlike their northern counterparts, cities like Atlanta, Dallas, and Houston have long promoted growth out and not up. These cities are full of sprawling suburbs and single-family homes, not densely concentrated skyscrapers and apartment buildings. What to do, then, when all those suburbanites need to get downtown for work? For a long time it seemed highways were the answer: twenty-lane–wide expanses of concrete that would allow commuters to move from home to work and back again. But these modern miracles have become time-sucking, pollution-spewing nightmares. The residents of these cities may not like it, but it's time for them to turn toward public transport like trains and buses if they want their cities to remain livable.

5. The organization of this passage can best be described as
   A) a comparison of two similar ideas.
   B) a description of a place.
   C) a discussion of several effects all related to the same cause.
   D) a discussion of a problem followed by a suggested solution.

Vocabulary

Reading questions may also ask you to figure out the meanings of words within passages. You may have never encountered some of these words before the test, but you can often use the same types of context clues you learned in the Verbal Reasoning chapter to find their meaning.

RESTATEMENT CLUES state the definition of the word in the sentence. The definition is often set apart from the rest of the sentence by a comma, parentheses, or a colon.

> Teachers often prefer teaching students with intrinsic motivation: these students have an internal desire to learn.
>
> The meaning of *intrinsic* is restated as *internal*.

CONTRAST CLUES include the opposite meaning of a word. Words like *but, on the other hand*, and *however* are tip-offs that a sentence contains a contrast clue.

> Janet was destitute after she lost her job, but her wealthy sister helped her get back on her feet.
>
> *Destitute* is contrasted with *wealthy*, so the definition of destitute is "poor."

POSITIVE/NEGATIVE CLUES tell you whether a word has a positive or negative meaning.

> The film was lauded by critics as stunning, and it was nominated for several awards.
>
> The positive descriptions *stunning* and *nominated for several awards* suggest that *lauded* has a positive meaning.

TEACHING TIPS: Cover the underlined word and have your student suggest words that would fit correctly in the blank. Then, have them look at the answers to see if any of the choices match their suggestions.

EXAMPLE

In December of 1944 Germany launched its last major offensive campaign of World War II, pushing through the dense forests of the Ardennes region of Belgium, France, and Luxembourg. The attack, designed to block the Allies from the Belgian port of Antwerp and to split their lines, caught the Allied forces by surprise. Due to troop positioning, the Americans bore the brunt of the attack, incurring 100,000 deaths, the highest number of casualties of any battle during the war. However, after a month of grueling fighting in the bitter cold, a lack of fuel and a masterful American military strategy resulted in an Allied victory that sealed Germany's fate.

6. In the last sentence, the word *grueling* most nearly means
   A) exhausting.
   B) expensive.
   C) intermittent.
   D) ineffective.

Style

POINT OF VIEW is the perspective the author writes from. A reading passage may be in the first, second, or third person.

▶ **FIRST PERSON:** a narrative is described from the writer's point of view (uses I, me, we, us).

▶ **SECOND PERSON:** a narrative addressing the reader directly as you; it is rarely used.

▶ **THIRD PERSON:** a narrative is described by somebody who isn't the writer (uses he, she, they, them).

The **TONE** of a passage describes the author's attitude toward the topic. The **MOOD** is the pervasive feeling or atmosphere in a passage that provokes specific emotions in the reader. Put simply, tone is how the author feels about the topic, and mood is how the reader feels about the text. In general, mood and tone can be categorized as positive, neutral, or negative.

TABLE 2.1. Words to Describe Tone and Mood

Positive	Neutral	Negative
admiring		angry
approving	casual	annoyed
celebratory	detached	belligerent
encouraging	formal	bitter
excited	impartial	condescending
funny		confused
hopeful		cynical

Positive	Neutral	Negative
humorous		depressed
optimistic		disrespectful
playful	informal	fearful
proud	objective	gloomy
respectful	questioning	melancholy
sentimental	unconcerned	pessimistic
silly		skeptical
sympathetic		unsympathetic

DICTION, or word choice, helps determine mood and tone in a passage. Many readers make the mistake of using the author's ideas alone to determine tone; a much better practice is to look at specific words and try to identify a pattern in the emotion they evoke. Does the writer choose positive words like *ambitious* and *confident*, which might be described as admiring? Or does she describe those concepts with negative words like *greedy* and *overbearing*, which might be described as disapproving?

When looking at tone, it's important to examine not just the dictionary definition of words. Many authors use **FIGURATIVE LANGUAGE**, which is the use of a word to imply something other than the word's literal definition. Common types of figurative language include:

- **SIMILE AND METAPHOR:** comparing two things (e.g., *I felt like a butterfly when I got a new haircut*)
- **HYPERBOLE:** exaggeration (e.g., I'm so tired I could sleep for three days)
- **VERBAL IRONY:** when the narrator says something that is the opposite of what he or she means
- **SITUATIONAL IRONY:** when something happens that is the opposite of what the reader expected
- **PERSONIFICATION:** when human characteristics are attributed to objects or animals

EXAMPLE

East River High School has released its graduation summary for the class of 2016. Out of a total of 558 senior students, 525 (94 percent) successfully completed their degree program and graduated. Of these, 402 (representing 72 percent of the total class) went on to attend a two- or four-year college or university. According to the data, the majority of East River High School's college-attending graduates chose a large, public institution.

7. Which of the following best describes the tone of the passage?
    A) professional
    B) casual
    C) concerned
    D) congratulatory

Putting It All Together

The passage and questions below will help you practice using everything you've learned in this chapter.

Have you ever wondered why exactly we feel pain when we get hurt? Or why some patients feel phantom pain even in the absence of a real trauma or damage? Pain is a highly sophisticated biological mechanism, one that is often downplayed or misinterpreted. Pain is much more than a measure of tissue damage—it is a complex neurological chain reaction that sends sensory data to the brain.

Pain is not produced by the toe you stubbed; rather, it is produced once the information about the "painful" incident reaches the brain. The brain analyzes the sensory signals emanating from the toe you stubbed, but the toe itself is not producing the sensation of pain.

In most cases, the brain offers accurate interpretations of the sensory data that is sent to it via the neurological processes in the body. If you hold your hand too close to a fire, for instance, the brain triggers pain that causes you to jerk your hand away, preventing further damage.

Phantom pain, most commonly associated with the amputation or loss of a limb, on the other hand, is triggered even in the absence of any injury. One possible explanation is that the spinal cord is still processing sensations from that area.

The science of pain management is complex and still poorly understood. However, anesthetics or anti-inflammatory medications can reduce or relieve pain by disrupting the neurological pathways that produce it. The absence of pain, however, is a double-edged sword—sometimes pain is the only clue to an underlying injury or disease. Likewise, an injury or disease can dull or eliminate pain, making it impossible to sense when something is actually wrong.

EXAMPLES

8. It can be inferred from the passage that people who cannot feel pain
    A) have damaged spinal cords.
    B) are more likely to injury themselves.
    C) will need to take anti-inflammatory medications.
    D) may still experience phantom pain.

9. In the fourth paragraph, "phantom pain" refers to pain that is
    A) imaginary.
    B) mild.
    C) associated with amputated limbs.
    D) caused by injury to hands and feet.

10. Which sentence best summarizes the passage's main idea?
- **A)** Many people wonder why people feel phantom pain.
- **B)** Pain is a complicated biological process, one that many people misjudge or do not understand.
- **C)** When you stub your toe, your brain analyzes the sensory signals coming from your injury.
- **D)** Anti-inflammatory medications can lessen or ease pain by affecting neurological processes.

11. According to the passage, what is true of phantom pain?
- **A)** It can be controlled with anesthetics or anti-inflammatory medications.
- **B)** Biologists do not know what causes this type of pain.
- **C)** It occurs because the body remembers how painful it felt when a limb was severely injured.
- **D)** It may happen because the spinal cord is still processing sensations from an amputated limb.

12. In the last paragraph, "a double-edged sword" means that the absence of pain can be
- **A)** positive or negative.
- **B)** mild or unbearable.
- **C)** caused by knife wounds.
- **D)** harder to endure than pain.

Answer Key

1. **D) is correct.** Choice A can be eliminated because it directly contradicts the rest of the passage. Choices B and C can also be eliminated because they state only specific details from the passage. While both choices contain details from the passage, neither is general enough to encompass the passage as a whole. Only Choice D provides an assertion that is both backed up by the passage's content and general enough to cover the entire passage.

2. **B) is correct.** The authors states that "children will face further illnesses in adulthood that are due to poor diet and lack of exercise." Choice A is incorrect because the author states that children should eat a diet rich in fruits and vegetables to prevent illness. Similarly, Choice C is wrong because the author is promoting cardiovascular exercise as healthy. The passage does not mention taking children to doctors.

3. **C) is correct.** The crowd's support for Alfie and their collective roar after the shot implies that Alfie scored the goal and won the championship.

4. **B) is correct.** The purpose of the passage is to persuade the reader of the author's opinion of the novel *Mockingjay,* specifically that the ending did not do the main character justice. The passage's use of the verb "argue" tells us that the author is presenting a case to the reader. The passage follows this statement with evidence—that the main character had a powerful personality.

5. **D) is correct.** Choice C is wrong because the author provides no root cause or a list of effects. Choices A and B are tricky because the passage contains structures similar to those described above. For example, it compares two things (cities in the North and South) and describes a place (a sprawling city). However, if you look at the overall organization of the passage, you can see that it starts by presenting a problem (transportation) and then suggests a solution (trains and buses), making Choice D the only option that encompasses the entire passage.

6. **A) is correct.** The context implies that the fighting was intense and tiring. The author describes the fight as lasting "a month" in the "bitter cold."

7. **A) is correct.** The passage is written in a neutral, professional tone. It does not include any informal, emotional, or first-person language.

8. **B) is correct.** In the final paragraph, the author states that a lack of pain can make it "impossible to sense when something is actually wrong," implying that people without pain will not know when they have an injury.

9. **C) is correct.** In the fourth paragraph, the author writes that phantom pain is "most commonly associated with the amputation or loss of a limb."

10. **B) is correct.** The passage is mainly about the fact that pain is a complicated process. The other sentences provide details from the passage.

11. **D) is correct.** In paragraph 3, the author writes, "Phantom pain [may be caused when] the spinal cord [continues to process] sensations from that area."

12. **A) is correct.** In the last paragraph, the author writes, "The absence of pain ... is a double-edged sword—sometimes pain is the only clue to an underlying injury or disease. Likewise, an injury or disease can dull or eliminate pain, making it impossible to sense when something is actually wrong." Readers can infer that the author is using the metaphor of a double-edged sword to show that the absence of pain is not always positive.

CHAPTER THREE
Mathematics

The ISEE includes two sections that measure mathematical abilities: mathematical achievement and quantitative reasoning. You will need to study the same concepts and skills for both sections. However, you will use your skills differently on each section.

The **MATHEMATICAL ACHIEVEMENT** section tests your ability to perform mathematical calculations. The answers to these questions will usually be values (like 37 inches or 50%) or expressions (like $x + 4$).

MATHEMATICAL ACHIEVEMENT QUESTION FORMAT

An electric company uses the formula $A = 0.057k + 23.50$, where k represents the number of kilowatt-hours used by the customer, to determine the amount of a customer's bill (A). Find the bill amount for a customer who uses 1210 kilowatt-hours.

- **A)** $45.47
- **B)** $70.31
- **C)** $92.47
- **D)** $713.20

Choice C is the correct answer. Substitute the value 1210 into the expression $0.057k + 23.50$ to find the amount of the bill:

$0.057k + 23.50 \rightarrow 0.057(1210) + 23.50$
$= 68.97 + 23.50 =$ **$92.47**

The **QUANTITATIVE REASONING** section focuses on mathematical thinking. You will not need to perform calculations in this section. Instead, you will be asked to think about the relationship between mathematical concepts. This section includes two types of questions: word problems and comparisons.

QUANTITATIVE WORD PROBLEMS will ask you to explain a mathematical concept in words. You may need to explain how you would solve a mathematical problem or show that you can manipulate formulas.

QUANTITATIVE REASONING (WORD PROBLEM) QUESTION FORMAT

A square has a side length of x meters. If 3 meters are added to its length and width, which statement is always true?

- **A)** The area of the square has increased by 9 m².
- **B)** The area of the square has increased by $6x$ m².
- **C)** The perimeter of the square has increased by 12 m.
- **D)** The perimeter of the square has increased by $3x$ m.

Choice C is the correct answer. The perimeter of the square was $4x$. The perimeter of the new square is $4(x + 3) = 4x + 12$. The perimeter of the square increased by 12 meters.

In **QUANTITATIVE COMPARISON QUESTIONS**, you will be asked to compare two quantities and choose which one is greater. The answer choices for these questions are always the same.

QUANTITATIVE REASONING (COMPARISONS) QUESTION FORMAT

Column A	Column B
x^3	x^{-3}

- **A)** The quantity in Column A is greater.
- **B)** The quantity in Column B is greater.
- **C)** The two quantities are equal.
- **D)** The relationship cannot be determined from the information given.

Choice D is the correct answer. The greater value cannot be determined without knowing the sign and value of x. For example, if $x = 4$, then Column A is the greater value. If $x = \frac{1}{4}$, then Column B is the greater value.

Numbers and Operations
ARITHMETIC OPERATIONS

The four basic arithmetic operations are addition, subtraction, multiplication, and division.

- ▶ **ADD** to combine two or more quantities ($6 + 5 = 11$).
- ▶ **SUBTRACT** to find the difference of two or more quantities ($10 - 3 = 7$).
- ▶ **MULTIPLY** to add a quantity multiple times ($4 \times 3 = 12 \Leftrightarrow 3 + 3 + 3 + 3 = 12$).
- ▶ **DIVIDE** to determine how many times one quantity goes into another ($10 \div 2 = 5$).

Word problems contain **CLUE WORDS** that help you determine which operation to use.

TABLE 3.1. Operations Word Problems

Operation	Clue Words	Example
Addition	sum together (in) total all in addition increased give	Leslie has 3 pencils. If her teacher **gives** her 2 pencils, how many does she now have **in total**? 3 + 2 = 5 pencils
Subtraction	minus less than take away decreased difference How many left? How many more/less?	Sean has 12 cookies. His sister **takes** 2 cookies. **How many** cookies does Sean have **left**? 12 − 2 = 10 cookies
Multiplication	product times of each/every groups of twice	A hospital department has 10 patient rooms. If **each** room holds 2 patients, how many patients can stay in the department? 10 × 2 = 20 patients
Division	divided per each/every distributed average How many for each? How many groups?	A teacher has 150 stickers to **distribute** to her class of 25 students. If each student gets the same number of stickers, **how many** stickers will **each** student get? 150 ÷ 25 = 6 stickers

EXAMPLE (MATHEMATICAL ACHIEVEMENT)

1. A case of pencils contains 10 boxes. Each box contains 150 pencils. How many pencils are in the case?

EXAMPLE (MATHEMATICAL ACHIEVEMENT)

2. Solve: $(12 - 8 \div 4)^2$

Mathematics

OPERATIONS WITH POSITIVE AND NEGATIVE NUMBERS

POSITIVE NUMBERS are greater than zero, and **NEGATIVE NUMBERS** are less than zero. Use the rules in Table 3.2 to determine the sign of the answer when performing operations with positive and negative numbers.

TABLE 3.2. Operations with Positive and Negative Numbers	
ADDITION AND SUBTRACTION	**MULTIPLICATION AND DIVISION**
positive + positive = positive $4 + 5 = 9$	positive × positive = positive $5 \times 3 = 15$
negative + negative = negative $-4 + (-5) = -9 \rightarrow -4 - 5 = -9$	negative × negative = positive $-6 \times (-5) = 30$
negative + positive = sign of the larger number $-15 + 9 = -6$	negative × positive = negative $-5 \times 4 = -20$

A **NUMBER LINE** shows numbers increasing from left to right (usually with zero in the middle). When adding positive and negative numbers, a number line can be used to find the sign of the answer. When adding a positive number, count to the right; when adding a negative number, count to the left. Note that adding a negative value is the same as subtracting.

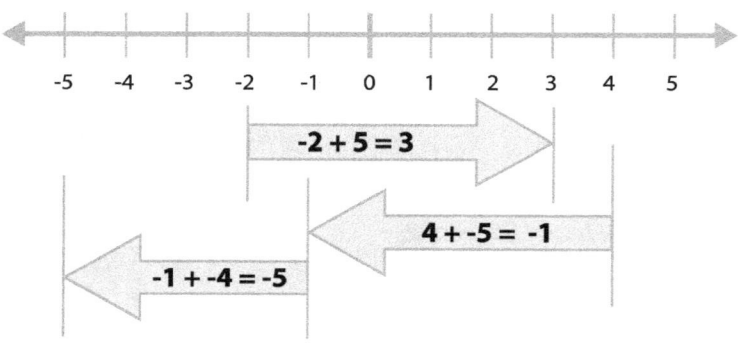

Figure 3.1. Adding Positive and Negative Numbers

EXAMPLE (MATHEMATICAL ACHIEVEMENT)

3. The wind chill on a cold day in January was −3°F. When the sun went down, the temperature fell 5°F. What was the temperature after the sun went down?

EXAMPLE (QUANTITATIVE REASONING)

4. Column A   Column B
   $-3 \times (-4)$ 3×4

   A) The quantity in Column A is greater.
   B) The quantity in Column B is greater.
   C) The two quantities are equal.
   D) The relationship cannot be determined from the information given.

EXPONENTS AND RADICALS

Exponential expressions, such as 5^3, contain a base and an exponent. The **EXPONENT** indicates how many times to use the **BASE** as a factor. In the expression 5^3, 5 is the base and 3 is the exponent. The value of 5^3 is found by multiplying 5 by itself 3 times: $5^3 = 5 \times 5 \times 5 = 125$. Rules for working with exponents are given in Table 3.3.

TABLE 3.3. Operations with Exponents

Rule	Example
$a^0 = 1$	$5^0 = 1$
$a^{-n} = \frac{1}{a^n}$	$5^{-3} = \frac{1}{5^3}$
$a^m a^n = a^{m+n}$	$5^3 5^4 = 5^{3+4} = 5^7$
$(a^m)^n = a^{m \times n}$	$(5^3)^4 = 5^{3(4)} = 5^{12}$
$\frac{a^m}{a^n} = a^{m-n}$	$\frac{5^4}{5^3} = 5^{4-3} = 5^1$
$(ab)^n = a^n b^n$	$(5 \times 6)^3 = 5^3 6^3$
$\left(\frac{a}{b}\right)^n = \frac{a^n}{b^n}$	$\left(\frac{5}{6}\right)^3 = \frac{5^3}{6^3}$
$\left(\frac{a}{b}\right)^{-n} = \left(\frac{b}{a}\right)^n$	$\left(\frac{5}{6}\right)^{-3} = \left(\frac{6}{5}\right)^3$
$\frac{a^{-m}}{b^{-n}} = \frac{b^n}{a^m}$	$\frac{5^{-3}}{6^{-4}} = \frac{6^4}{5^3}$

Finding the **ROOT** of a number is the inverse of raising a number to a power. In other words, the root is the number of times a value should be multiplied by itself to reach a given value. Roots are named for the power on the base:

▸ 5 is the **SQUARE ROOT** of 25 because $5^2 = 25$
▸ 5 is the **CUBE ROOT** of 125 because $5^3 = 125$
▸ 5 is the **FOURTH ROOT** of 625, because $5^4 = 625$

The symbol for finding the root of a number is the radical: $\sqrt{\blacksquare}$. By itself, the radical indicates a square root: $\sqrt{36} = 6$ because $6^2 = 36$. Other numbers can be included in

Mathematics 27

front of the radical to indicate different roots: $\sqrt[4]{1{,}296}$ because $6^4 = 1{,}296$. The number under the radical is called the **RADICAND**. Rules for working with radicals are given in Table 3.4.

TABLE 3.4. Operations with Radicals

Rule	Example
$\sqrt[b]{ac} = \sqrt[b]{a}\sqrt[b]{c}$	$\sqrt[3]{81} = \sqrt[3]{27}\sqrt[3]{3} = 3\sqrt[3]{3}$
$\sqrt[b]{\frac{a}{c}} = \frac{\sqrt[b]{a}}{\sqrt[b]{c}}$	$\sqrt{\frac{4}{81}} = \frac{\sqrt{4}}{\sqrt{81}} = \frac{2}{9}$
$\sqrt[b]{a^c} = (\sqrt[b]{a})^c = a^{\frac{c}{b}}$	$\sqrt[3]{6^2} = (\sqrt[3]{6})^2 = 6^{\frac{2}{3}}$

EXAMPLE (MATHEMATICAL ACHIEVEMENT)

5. Simplify: Determine the largest square number that is a factor of the radicand, $\sqrt{48}$. Write the radicand as a product using that square number as a factor.

EXAMPLE (QUANTITATIVE REASONING)

6. Column A   Column B
   $\sqrt{x}$ $x^{(1/3)}$

   A) The quantity in Column A is greater.
   B) The quantity in Column B is greater.
   C) The two quantities are equal.
   D) The relationship cannot be determined from the information given.

SCIENTIFIC NOTATION

SCIENTIFIC NOTATION is a method of representing very large and very small numbers in the form $a \times 10^n$, where a is a value between 1 and 10, and n is a nonzero integer. For example, the number 927,000,000 is written in scientific notation as 9.27×10^8. The rules of exponents are used to perform operations with numbers in scientific notation.

- When adding and subtracting numbers in scientific notation, write all numbers with the same n value and add or subtract the a values.
- When multiplying numbers in scientific notation, multiply the a values and add the n values (exponents).
- To divide numbers in scientific notation, divide the a values and subtract the n values (exponents).

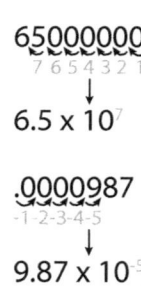

Figure 3.2. Scientific Notation

EXAMPLE (MATHEMATICAL ACHIEVEMENT)

7. Simplify: $(3.8 \times 10^3) + (4.7 \times 10^2)$

___

EXAMPLE (QUANTITATIVE REASONING)

8. **Column A**   **Column B**
   3.8×10^{-3} 1.2×10^{-2}
   - A) The quantity in Column A is greater.
   - B) The quantity in Column B is greater.
   - C) The two quantities are equal.
   - D) The relationship cannot be determined from the information given.

ORDER OF OPERATIONS

When performing multiple operations, the **ORDER OF OPERATIONS** must be used to obtain the correct answer. The problem should be worked in the following order:

Please **E**xcuse (**M**y **D**ear) (**A**unt **S**ally)

1. **P** — Parentheses: Calculate expressions inside parentheses, brackets, braces, etc.
2. **E** — Exponents: Calculate exponents and square roots.
3. **M** — Multiply and **D** — Divide: Calculate any remaining multiplication and division in order from left to right.
4. **A** — Add and **S** — Subtract: Calculate any remaining addition and subtraction in order from left to right.

The steps "Multiply/Divide" and "Add/Subtract" are completed from left to right. In other words, divide before multiplying if the division is to the left of the multiplication.

For example, the expression $(3^2 - 2)^2 + (4)5^3$ is simplified using the following steps:

1. Parentheses: Because the parentheses in this problem contain two operations (exponents and subtraction), use the order of operations within the parentheses. Exponents come before subtraction.
   $(3^2 - 2)^2 + (4)5^3 = (9 - 2)^2 + (4)5^3 = (7)^2 + (4)5^3$
2. Exponents: $(7)^2 + (4)5^3 = 49 + (4)125$
3. Multiplication and division: $49 + (4)125 = 49 + 500$
4. Addition and subtraction: $49 + 500 = 549$

TEACHING TIP: When working with complicated expressions, ask your student to underline or highlight the operation being performed in each step to avoid confusion.

EXAMPLE (MATHEMATICAL ACHIEVEMENT)

9. Simplify: $-3^2 + 4(5) + (5 - 6)^2 - 8$

EXAMPLE (QUANTITATIVE REASONING)

10. Column A   Column B
    6 − (2 × 3)   (6 − 2) × 3

    A) The quantity in Column A is greater.
    B) The quantity in Column B is greater.
    C) The two quantities are equal.
    D) The relationship cannot be determined from the information given.

FRACTIONS

A **FRACTION** represents parts of a whole. The top number of a fraction, called the **NUMERATOR**, indicates how many equal-sized parts are present. The bottom number of a fraction, called the **DENOMINATOR**, indicates how many equal-sized parts make a whole.

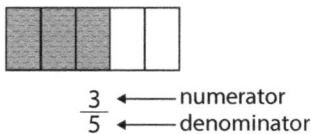

Figure 3.3. Parts of Fractions

Fractions have several forms:

▶ **PROPER FRACTION:** the numerator is less than the denominator

▶ **IMPROPER FRACTION:** the numerator is greater than or equal to the denominator

▶ **MIXED NUMBER:** the combination of a whole number and a fraction

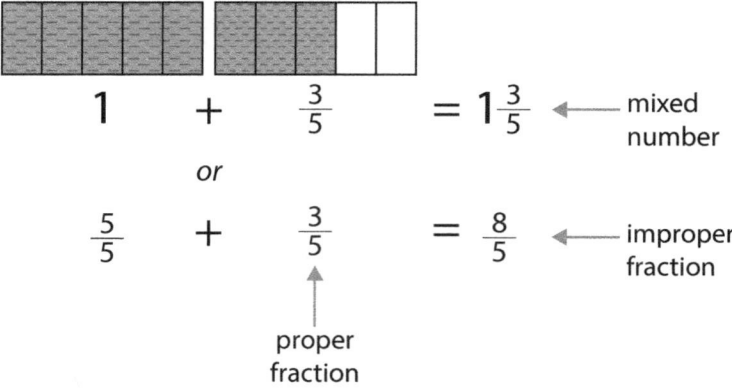

Figure 3.4. Types of Fractions

Improper fractions can be converted to mixed numbers by dividing. In fact, the fraction bar is also a division symbol.

$$\frac{14}{3} = 14 \div 3 = 4 \text{ (with 2 left over)}$$
$$143 = 423 \; \frac{14}{3} = 4\frac{2}{3}$$

To convert a mixed number to a fraction, multiply the whole number by the denominator of the fraction, and add the numerator. The result becomes the numerator of the improper fraction; the denominator remains the same.

$$5\frac{2}{3} = \frac{(5 \times 3) + 2}{3} = \frac{17}{3}$$

To **MULTIPLY FRACTIONS**, multiply numerators and multiply denominators. Reduce the product to lowest terms. To **DIVIDE FRACTIONS**, multiply the first fraction by the reciprocal of the second fraction. (The **RECIPROCAL** of a fraction is just the fraction with the top and bottom numbers switched.) When multiplying and dividing mixed numbers, the mixed numbers must be converted to improper fractions.

$$\frac{a}{b} \times \frac{c}{d} = \frac{ac}{bd}$$
$$\frac{a}{b} \div \frac{c}{d} = \left(\frac{a}{b}\right)\left(\frac{d}{c}\right) = \frac{ad}{bc}$$

Adding or subtracting fractions requires a common denominator. To find a **COMMON DENOMINATOR**, multiply the denominators of the fractions. Then, to add the fractions, add the numerators and keep the denominator the same.

$$\frac{a}{b} + \frac{c}{b} = \frac{a+c}{b}$$
$$\frac{a}{b} - \frac{c}{b} = \frac{a-c}{b}$$

EXAMPLE (MATHEMATICAL ACHIEVEMENT)

11. Ari and Teagan each ordered a pizza. Ari has $\frac{1}{4}$ of his pizza left, and Teagan has $\frac{1}{3}$ of her pizza left. How much total pizza do they have left?

_____

EXAMPLE (QUANTITATIVE REASONING)

12. Column A   Column B
     $4\frac{3}{4}$ $\frac{38}{8}$

- **A)** The quantity in Column A is greater.
- **B)** The quantity in Column B is greater.
- **C)** The two quantities are equal.
- **D)** The relationship cannot be determined from the information given.

DECIMALS

In the base-10 system, each digit (the numeric symbols 0 – 9) in a number is worth ten times as much as the number to the right of it. For example, in the number 321 each digit has a different value based on its position: $321 = 300 + 20 + 1$. The value of each place is called **PLACE VALUE**.

TABLE 3.5. Place Value Chart

1,000,000	100,000	10,000	1,000	100	10	1		$\frac{1}{10}$	$\frac{1}{100}$
10^6	10^5	10^4	10^3	10^2	10^1	10^0	.	10^{-1}	10^{-2}
millions	hundred thousands	ten thousands	thousands	hundreds	tens	ones	decimal	tenths	hundredths

Decimals can be added, subtracted, multiplied, and divided:

▶ To add or subtract decimals, align at the decimal point, and perform the operation. Keep the decimal point in the same place in the answer.

▶ To multiply decimals, multiply the numbers without the decimal points. Add the number of decimal places to the right of the decimal point in the original numbers. Place the decimal point in the answer so that there are that many places to the right of the decimal.

▶ When dividing decimals, move the decimal point to the right in order to make the divisor a whole number. Move the decimal the same number of places in the dividend. Divide the numbers without regard to the decimal. Then, place the decimal point of the quotient directly above the decimal point of the dividend.

TEACHING TIP: To determine which way to move the decimal after multiplying, remember that changing the decimal should always make the final answer smaller.

EXAMPLE (MATHEMATICAL ACHIEVEMENT)

13. A customer at a restaurant ordered a drink that cost $2.20, a meal that cost $32.54, and a dessert that cost $4. How much was the total bill?

EXAMPLE (QUANTITATIVE REASONING)

14. George has $7.24 in coins.

Column A
the number of pennies George has

Column B
the number of dimes George has

A) The quantity in Column A is greater.
B) The quantity in Column B is greater.
C) The two quantities are equal.
D) The relationship cannot be determined from the information given.

RATIOS AND PROPORTIONS

A **RATIO** is a comparison of two quantities. For example, if a class consists of 15 women and 10 men, the ratio of women to men is 15 to 10. This ratio can also be written as 15:10 or $\frac{15}{10}$. Ratios, like fractions, can be reduced by dividing by common factors.

A **PROPORTION** is a statement that two ratios are equal. For example, the proportion $\frac{5}{10} = \frac{7}{14}$ is true because both ratios are equal to $\frac{1}{2}$.

The cross product is found by multiplying the numerator of one fraction by the denominator of the other (*across* the equal sign).

Cross product: $\frac{a}{b} = \frac{c}{d} \Rightarrow ad = bc$

The fact that the cross products of proportions are equal can be used to solve proportions in which one of the values is missing. Use *x* to represent the missing value, then cross multiply and solve.

$$\frac{5}{x} = \frac{7}{14}$$

$5(14) = x(7)$

$70 = 7x$

$x = 10$

EXAMPLE (MATHEMATICAL ACHIEVEMENT)

15. The dosage for a particular medication is proportional to the weight of the patient. If the dosage for a patient weighing 60 kg is 90 mg, what is the dosage for a patient weighing 80 kg?

EXAMPLE (MATHEMATICAL ACHIEVEMENT)

16. Jacob is running for class president at his high school. There were 250 students, 40% of the students, who voted for him. How many students are in Jacob's class?

PERCENTS

A **PERCENT** (or percentage) means *per hundred* and is expressed with the percent symbol, %. For example, 54% means 54 out of 100. Percentages are converted to decimals by moving the decimal point two places to the left; 54% = 0.54. Percentages can be solved by setting up a proportion:

$$\frac{\text{part}}{\text{whole}} = \frac{\%}{100}$$

PERCENT CHANGE involves a change from an original amount. Often percent change problems appear as word problems that include discounts, growth, or markups. In order to solve percent change problems, it is necessary to identify the percent change (as a decimal), the amount of change, and the original amount. (Keep in mind that one of these will be the value being solved for.) These values can then be substituted in the equations below:

$$\text{amount of change} = \text{original amount} \times \text{percent change}$$

$$\text{percent change} = \frac{\text{amount of change}}{\text{original amount}}$$

$$\text{original amount} = \frac{\text{amount of change}}{\text{percent change}}$$

EXAMPLES (MATHEMATICAL ACHIEVEMENT)

17. On Tuesday, a radiology clinic had 80% of patients come in for their scheduled appointments. If they saw 16 patients, how many scheduled appointments did the clinic have on Tuesday?

18. A smart HDTV that originally cost $1500 is on sale for 45% off. What is the sale price for the item?

19. Kevin is planning a party and can host 120 people. If he sends out invitations to his friends and expects 30% to decline, what is the maximum number of invitations he should send?

ESTIMATION AND ROUNDING

ESTIMATION is the process of rounding numbers before performing operations to make operations easier. Estimation can be used when an exact answer is not necessary or to check work.

To **ROUND** a number, first identify the digit in the specified place value. Then look at the digit one place to the right. If that digit is 4 or less, keep the digit in the specified place value the same. If that digit is 5 or more, add 1 to the digit in the specified place value. All the digits to the right of the specified place value become zeros.

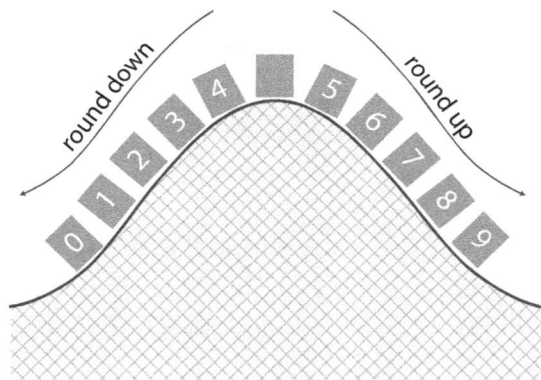

Figure 3.5. Rounding

EXAMPLE (MATHEMATICAL ACHIEVEMENT)

20. Voter turnout in a city election is estimated to be 80%. If Hank earns 4000 or 40% of the vote, how many registered voters live in the city? (Round to the nearest 100.)

EXAMPLE (QUANTITATIVE REASONING)

21. The populations of five local towns are given below. Find the total population to the nearest 1000 people.

TOWN	POPULATION
A	12,341
B	8975
C	9431
D	10,521
E	11,427

MATRICES

A **MATRIX** is a rectangular arrangement of numbers into **ROWS** (horizontal set of numbers) and **COLUMNS** (vertical set of numbers). A matrix with the same number of rows and columns is called a **SQUARE MATRIX**.

The **DIMENSIONS** of a matrix are given as $m \times n$, where m is the number of rows and n is the number of columns.

$$A = \begin{bmatrix} 1 & 8 & -2 \\ -12 & -3 & 7 \end{bmatrix}$$

Figure 3.6. Parts of a Matrix

When the matrices have the same dimensions, the values in corresponding positions in the matrices can be added or subtracted.

$$\begin{bmatrix} a & b \\ c & d \end{bmatrix} \pm \begin{bmatrix} e & f \\ g & h \end{bmatrix} = \begin{bmatrix} a \pm e & b \pm f \\ c \pm g & d \pm h \end{bmatrix}$$

Matrices can be multiplied by a single value called a scalar. To perform this operation, each value in the matrix is multiplied by the scalar.

$$x \begin{bmatrix} a & b \\ c & d \end{bmatrix} = \begin{bmatrix} xa & xb \\ xc & xd \end{bmatrix}$$

EXAMPLE (MATHEMATICAL ACHIEVEMENT)

22. Simplify:

$$\begin{bmatrix} 7 & 4 & 1 \\ -6 & 3 & 5 \end{bmatrix} + \begin{bmatrix} 2 & -8 & 5 \\ -1 & 0 & 4 \end{bmatrix}$$

EXAMPLE (MATHEMATICAL ACHIEVEMENT)

23. Simplify:

$$2 \begin{bmatrix} 6 & -3 \\ 4 & 10 \end{bmatrix}$$

COMBINATIONS AND PERMUTATIONS

Combinations and permutations describe how many ways a number of objects can be arranged. The total number of objects in the set is written as n, and the number of objects to be arranged is represented by r (or k). In a **COMBINATION**, the order of the selections does not matter because every available slot to be filled is the same. Examples of combinations include:

- picking 3 people from a group of 12 to form a committee (220 possible committees)
- picking 3 pizza toppings from 10 options (120 possible pizzas)

In a **PERMUTATION**, the order of the selection matters, meaning each available slot is different. Examples of permutations include:

- handing out gold, silver, and bronze medals in a race with 100 participants (970,200 possible options)
- selecting a president, vice president, secretary, and treasurer from among a committee of 12 people (11,880 possible options)

The formulas for both calculations are similar. The only difference is the $r!$ in the denominator of a combination, which accounts for redundant outcomes. Note that both permutations and combinations can be written in several different shortened notations.

Permutation: $P(n, r) = {}_nP_r = \dfrac{n!}{(n-r)!}$

Combination: $C(n, r) = {}_nC_r = \binom{n}{r} = \dfrac{n!}{(n-r)!r!}$

> **TEACHING TIP:**
> To calculate a factorial (r!), multiply all the whole numbers from 1 to r!. For example: 5! = 5 × 4 × 3 × 2 × 1 = 120.

EXAMPLE (MATHEMATICAL ACHIEVEMENT)

24. If there are 20 applicants for 3 open positions, how many different ways can a team of 3 be hired?

EXAMPLE (MATHEMATICAL ACHIEVEMENT)

25. Calculate the number of unique permutations that can be made with five of the letters in the word *pickle*.

SEQUENCES AND SERIES

A **SEQUENCE** is a string of numbers (called terms) that follow a specific pattern. The terms in a sequence are numbered (meaning there is a first term, a second term, and so on) and are generally described with the notation a_n where n is the number of the term.

In an **ARITHMETIC SEQUENCE**, the difference between each term is the same (a value called the **COMMON DIFFERENCE**). For example, the sequence {20, 30, 40, 50} is arithmetic because the difference between the terms is 10. To find the next term in an arithmetic sequence, add the common value to the previous term.

$$a_n = a_1 + (n-1)d$$

where d is the common difference

In a **GEOMETRIC SEQUENCE**, the ratio between consecutive terms is constant (a value called the **COMMON RATIO**). For example, the sequence {2, 4, 8, 16, 32, 64} is geometric with a common ratio of 2. To find the common ratio, choose any term in the sequence and divide it by the previous term. To find the next term in the sequence, multiply the previous term by the common ratio.

$$a_n = a_1 r^n - 1$$

where r is the common ratio

EXAMPLE (MATHEMATICAL ACHIEVEMENT)

26. Find the sixth term of the following arithmetic sequence: −57, −40, −23, −6, …

EXAMPLE (QUANTITATIVE REASONING)

27. **Column A**
The 100th term of an arithmetic sequence with a common difference of 6 where the first term is 2.

Column B
The 100th term of a geometric sequence with a common ratio of 6 where the first term is 2.

- **A)** The quantity in Column A is greater.
- **B)** The quantity in Column B is greater.
- **C)** The two quantities are equal.
- **D)** The relationship cannot be determined from the information given.

Algebra

EVALUATING EXPRESSIONS

The foundation of algebra is the **VARIABLE**, an unknown number represented by a symbol (usually a letter such as x or a). Variables can be preceded by a **COEFFICIENT**, which is a constant in front of the variable, such as $4x$ or $-2a$. An **ALGEBRAIC EXPRESSION** is any sum, difference, product, or quotient of variables and numbers (for example, $3x^2$, $2x + 7y - 1$, and $5/x$ are all algebraic expressions). The value of an expression is found by replacing the variable with a given value and simplifying the result.

EXAMPLE (MATHEMATICAL ACHIEVEMENT)

28. Evaluate the following expression for $a = -10$:
$\frac{a^2}{4} - 3a + 4$

EXAMPLE (QUANTITATIVE REASONING)

29. Evaluate the following expression for $a = xy$ and $b = x^2$:
$2a + 3b$

ADDING AND SUBTRACTING ALGEBRAIC EXPRESSIONS

TERMS are any quantities that are added or subtracted in an expression. For example, the terms of the expression $x^2 + 5$ are x^2 and 5. **LIKE TERMS** are terms with the same variable part. For example, in the expression $2x + 3xy - 2z + 6y + 2xy$, the like terms are $3xy$ and $2xy$.

Expressions can be added or subtracted by simply adding and subtracting like terms. The other terms in the expression will not change.

$2x + \underline{3xy} - 2z + 6y + \underline{2xy} \rightarrow 2x - 2z + 6y + (\underline{3xy} + \underline{2xy}) \rightarrow 2x - 2z + 6y + \underline{5xy}$

EXAMPLE (MATHEMATICAL ACHIEVEMENT)

30. Simplify the expression: $4x - 3y + 12z + 2x - 7y - 10z$

EXAMPLE (QUANTITATIVE REASONING)

31. At the arcade, games give out green tickets or red tickets. The arcade also gives out small boxes to store tickets. Paul and Paula both play numerous games, and at the end of the day, Paul has 3 boxes of green tickets and 8 boxes of red tickets, while Paula has 6 boxes of green tickets and 2 boxes of red tickets. If the green box holds g tickets and the red box hold r tickets, write an expression that describes how many tickets they have together.

DISTRIBUTING AND FACTORING

Often, simplifying expressions requires distributing and factoring, which are opposite processes. To **DISTRIBUTE**, multiply the term outside the parentheses by each term inside the parentheses. For each term, coefficients are multiplied, and exponents are added (following the rules of exponents).

$$2x(3x^2 + 7) = 6x^3 + 14x$$

FACTORING is the reverse process: taking a polynomial and writing it as a product of two or more factors. The first step in factoring a polynomial is always to "undistribute," or factor out, the greatest common factor (GCF) among the terms. The remaining terms are placed in parentheses. Factoring can be checked by multiplying the GCF through the parentheses.

$$14a^2 + 7a = 7a(2a + 1)$$

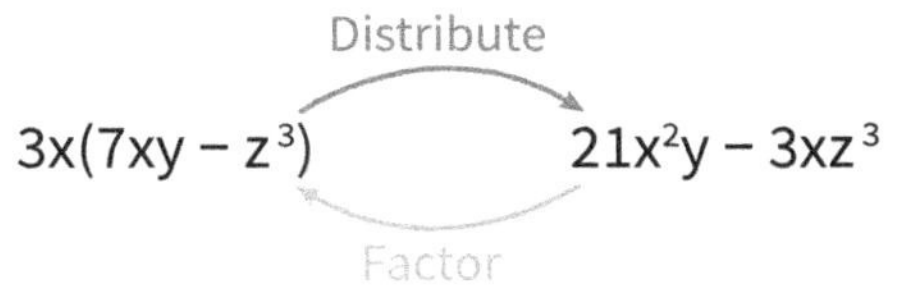

$$3x(7xy - z^3) \xrightarrow{\text{Distribute}} 21x^2y - 3xz^3$$
$$\xleftarrow{\text{Factor}}$$

Figure 3.7. Distribution and Factoring

To multiply binomials (expressions with two terms), use FOIL: First – Outer – Inner – Last. Multiply the first term in each expression, the outer terms, the inner terms, and the last term in each expression. Then simplify the expression.

$$(2x + 3)(x - 4)$$
$$= (2x)(x) + (2x)(-4) + (3)(x) + 3(-4)$$
$$= 2x^2 - 8x + 3x - 12$$
$$= 2x^2 - 5x - 12$$

EXAMPLE (MATHEMATICAL ACHIEVEMENT)

32. Expand the following expression: $5x(x^2 - 2c + 10)$

EXAMPLE (QUANTITATIVE REASONING)

33. Given $x > y > 0$,

    Column A   **Column B**
    $4x - 2y + 2x - 10$ $2(3x - y - 5)$

    A) The quantity in Column A is greater.

    B) The quantity in Column B is greater.

    C) The two quantities are equal.

    D) The relationship cannot be determined from the information given.

EQUATIONS

An **EQUATION** states that two expressions are equal to each other. Solving an equation means finding the value(s) of the variable that make the equation true. To solve a linear equation (which has two variables with no exponents), manipulate the terms so that the variable being solved for is isolated on one side of the equal sign. All other terms should be on the other side of the equal sign.

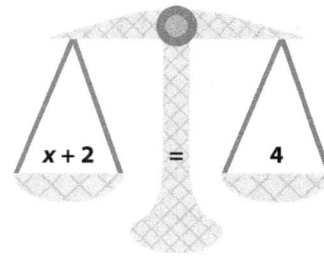

Figure 3.8. Equations

The way to solve linear equations is to "undo" all the operations that connect numbers to the variable of interest. Follow these steps:

1. Eliminate fractions by multiplying each side by the least common multiple of any denominators.

2. Distribute to eliminate parentheses, braces, and brackets.

3. Combine like terms.

4. Use addition or subtraction to collect all terms containing the variable of interest to one side and all terms not containing the variable to the other side.

5. Use multiplication or division to remove coefficients from the variable being solved for.

> **TEACHING TIP:**
> Use tactile objects to demonstrate equality. Divide the objects into two groups and have students add or subtract the same number of objects from each group. Point out that as long as the same action is performed on both sides, the two groups remain equal.

$2(2x - 8) = x + 7$	
$4x - 16 = x + 7$	Distribute.
$4x - 16 - x = x + 7 - x$ $3x - 16 = -7$	Subtract x to isolate the variable on one side.
$3x - 16 + 16 = -7 + 16$ $3x = 9$	Add 16 to both sides.
$\frac{3x}{3} = \frac{9}{3}$ $x = 3$	Divide both sides by 3.

40   ISEE Upper Level Test Prep

EXAMPLE (MATHEMATICAL ACHIEVEMENT)

34. Solve for x: $5(x + 3) - 12 = 43$

EXAMPLE (MATHEMATICAL ACHIEVEMENT)

35. Mandy babysits for families and charges $8 an hour for one child plus $3 an hour per additional child. The Buxton family has 4 children, and they ask Mandy to babysit for 5 hours. How much will Mandy make for babysitting the Buxton children?

INEQUALITIES

INEQUALITIES are similar to equations, except both sides of the problem are not necessarily equal ($\neq$). Inequalities may be represented as follows:

- greater than (>)
- greater than or equal to (≥)
- less than (<)
- less than or equal to (≤)

Inequalities may be represented on a number line, as shown below. A circle is placed on the end point with a filled circle representing ≤ and ≥ and an empty circle representing < and >. An arrow is then drawn to show either all the values greater than or less than the value circled.

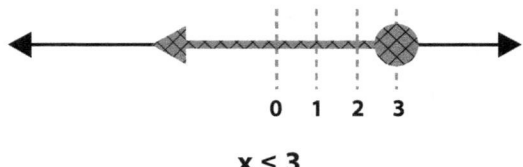

$x \leq 3$

Figure 3.9. Inequality Line Graph

Inequalities can be solved by manipulating, just like equations. The only difference is that the direction of the inequality sign must be reversed when the inequality is divided by a negative number.

$$10 - 2x > 14$$
$$-2x > 4$$
$$x < -2$$

The solution to an inequality is a *set* of numbers, not a single value. For example, simplifying $4x + 2 \leq 14$ gives the inequality $x \leq 3$, meaning every number less than or equal to 3 would be included in the set of correct answers.

EXAMPLE (MATHEMATICAL ACHIEVEMENT)

36. Solve the inequality: $4x + 10 > 58$

EXAMPLE (QUANTITATIVE REASONING)

37. The students on the track team are buying new uniforms. Shirts cost $12, pants cost $15, and a pair of shoes costs $45. If the team has a budget of $2500, write a mathematical sentence that represents how many of each item they can buy.

GRAPHING LINEAR EQUATIONS ON A COORDINATE PLANE

A **COORDINATE PLANE** is a plane containing the x- and y-axes. The **X-AXIS** is the horizontal line on a graph where $y = 0$. The **Y-AXIS** is the vertical line on a graph where $x = 0$. The x-axis and y-axis intersect to create four **QUADRANTS**. The first quadrant is in the upper right, and other quadrants are labeled counterclockwise using the roman numerals I, II, III, and IV. **POINTS**, or locations, on the graph are written as **ORDERED PAIRS**, (x, y), with the point $(0, 0)$ called the **ORIGIN**. Points are plotted by counting over x places from the origin horizontally and y places from the origin vertically.

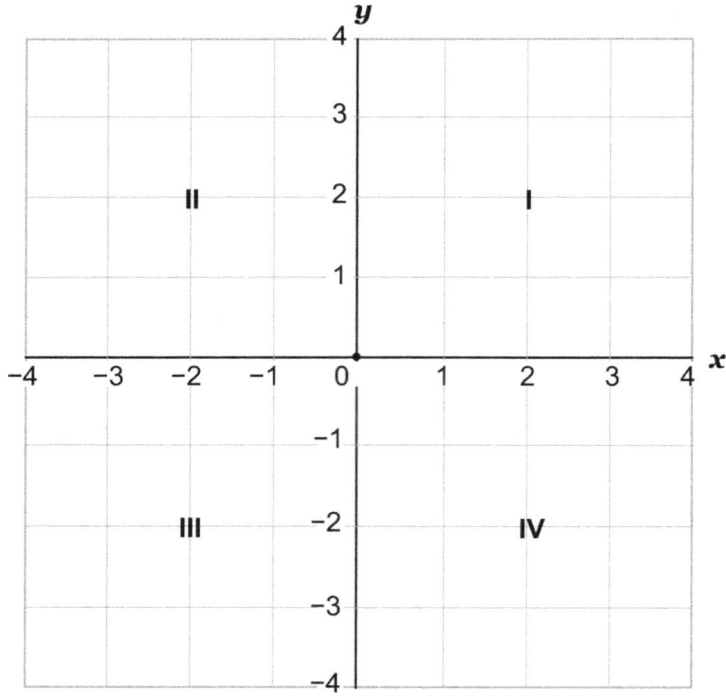

Figure 3.10. Four Quadrants

The most common way to write a linear equation is **SLOPE-INTERCEPT FORM**:

$$y = mx + b$$

In this equation, m is the slope, and b is the y-intercept. The **Y-INTERCEPT** is the point where the line crosses the y-axis, or where x equals zero. **SLOPE** is often described as "rise over run" because it is calculated as the difference in y-values (rise) over the difference in x-values (run).

> **TEACHING TIP:**
> Use the phrase begin, move to remember that b is the y-intercept (where to begin) and m is the slope (how the line moves).

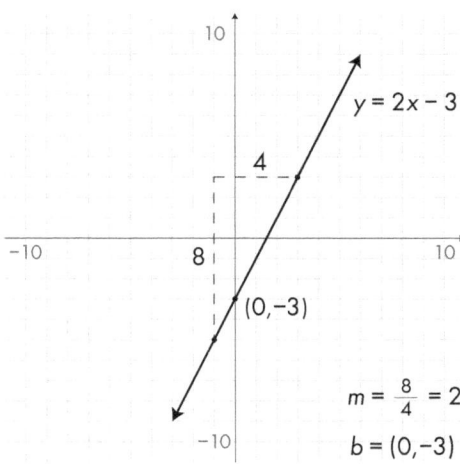

Figure 3.11. Linear Equation

$$m = \frac{y_2 - y_1}{x_2 - x_1} = \frac{\text{rise}}{\text{run}}$$

To graph a linear equation, identify the y-intercept and place that point on the y-axis. Then, starting at the y-intercept, use the slope of "rise over run" to go "up and over" and place the next point. The numerator of the slope tells you how many units to go up, the "rise." The denominator of the slope tells you how many units to go to the right, the "run." However, if the slope is negative, reverse the process and go down and over to the left before placing the next point. You can repeat the process to plot additional points. These points can then be connected to draw the line. To find the equation of a line, identify the y-intercept, if possible, on the graph and use two easily identifiable points to find the slope.

EXAMPLE (MATHEMATICAL ACHIEVEMENT)

38. What is the slope of the line whose equation is $6x - 2y - 8 = 0$?

EXAMPLE (QUANTITATIVE REASONING)

39. In which quadrant is the point $(-5, 2)$ located?

Geometry and Measurement

UNITS

The United States uses *customary units*, sometimes called *standard units*. In this system, several different units can be used to describe the same variable. These units and the relationships between them are shown in Table 3.6.

TABLE 3.6. US Customary Units

Variable Measured	Unit	Conversions
Length	inches, foot, yard, mile	12 inches = 1 foot 3 feet = 1 yard 5280 feet = 1 mile
Weight	ounces, pound, ton	16 ounces = 1 pound 2000 pounds = 1 ton
Volume	fluid ounces, cup, pint, quart, gallon	8 fluid ounces = 1 cup 2 cups = 1 pint 2 pints = 1 quart 4 quarts = 1 gallon
Time	second, minute, hour, day	60 seconds = 1 minute 60 minutes = 1 hour 24 hours = 1 day
Area	square inch, square foot, square yard	144 square inches = 1 square foot 9 square feet = 1 square yard

Most other countries use the metric system, which has its own set of units for variables like length, weight, and volume. These units are modified by prefixes that make large and small numbers easier to handle. These units and prefixes are shown in Table 3.7.

TABLE 3.7. Metric Units and Prefixes

Variable Measured	Base Unit
length	meter
weight	gram
volume	liter

Metric Prefix	Conversion
kilo	base unit × 1000
hecto	base unit × 100
deka	base unit × 10
deci	base unit × 0.1
centi	base unit × 0.01
milli	base unit × 0.001

Conversion factors are used to convert one unit to another (either within the same system or between different systems). A conversion factor is simply a fraction built from two equivalent values. For example, there are 12 inches in 1 foot, so the conversion factor is $\frac{12 \text{ in}}{1 \text{ ft}}$ or $\frac{1 \text{ ft}}{12 \text{ in}}$.

To convert from one unit to another, multiply the original value by a conversion factor. Choose a conversion factor that will eliminate the unwanted unit with the desired unit.

How many inches are in 6 feet?

$$\frac{6 \text{ ft} \times 12 \text{ in}}{1 \text{ ft}} = \frac{6 \text{ ft} \times 12 \text{ in}}{1 \text{ ft}} = 72 \text{ in}$$

EXAMPLE (MATHEMATICAL ACHIEVEMENT)

40. How many centimeters are in 2.5 m?

EXAMPLE (QUANTITATIVE REASONING)

41. **Column A** **Column B**
3 kilometers   300 dekameters

- **A)** The quantity in Column A is greater.
- **B)** The quantity in Column B is greater.
- **C)** The two quantities are equal.
- **D)** The relationship cannot be determined from the information given.

GEOMETRIC FIGURES

Geometric Figures are shapes made up of points, lines, or planes. A **point** is simply a location in space; it does not have any dimensional properties like length, area, or volume. A collection of points that extend infinitely in both directions is a **line**, and one that extends infinitely in only one direction is a **RAY**. A section of a line with a beginning and end point is a **LINE SEGMENT**. Lines, rays, and line segments are examples of **ONE-DIMENSIONAL** objects because they can only be measured in one dimension (length).

Figure 3.12. One-Dimensional Object

Lines, rays, and line segments can intersect to create **ANGLES**, which are measured in degrees or radians. Angles between 0° and 90° are **ACUTE**, and angles between 90° and 180° are **OBTUSE**. An angle of exactly 90° is a **RIGHT ANGLE**, and two lines that form right angles are **PERPENDICULAR**. Lines that do not intersect are described as **PARALLEL**. Any two angles whose sum is 90° are called **COMPLEMENTARY ANGLES**. **SUPPLEMENTARY ANGLES** have a sum of 180°.

TEACHING TIP:
Parallel lines have the same or equal slopes. The slopes of two perpendicular lines are negative reciprocals of each other.

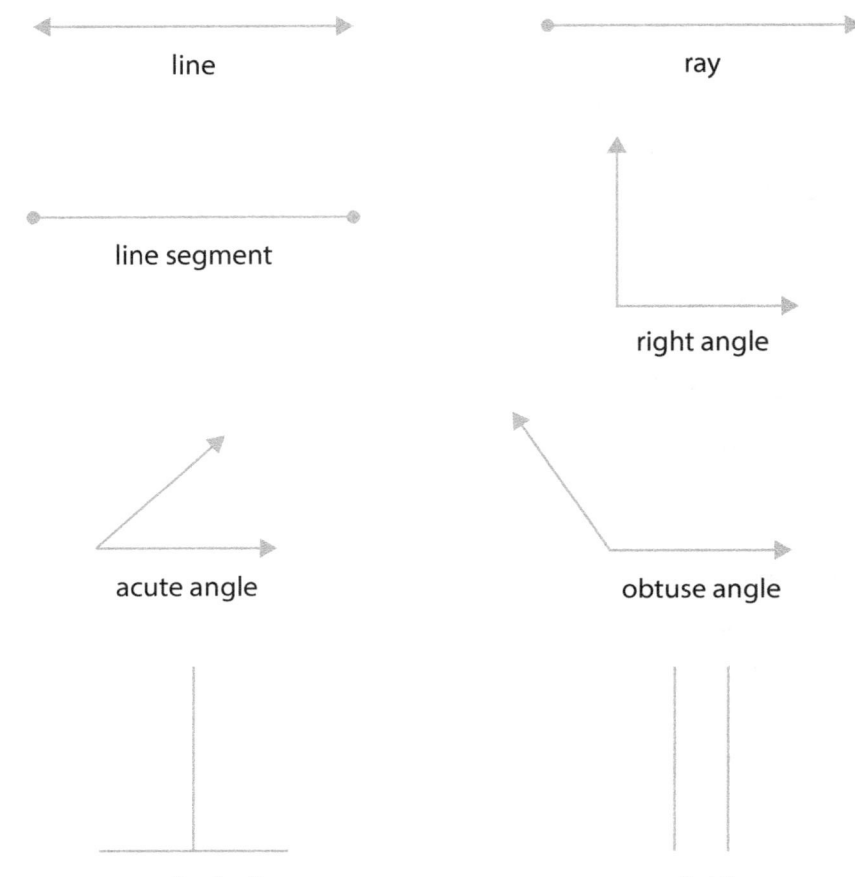

Figure 3.13. Lines and Angles

TWO-DIMENSIONAL objects can be measured in two dimensions (length and width). A **PLANE** is a two-dimensional object that extends infinitely.

Figure 3.14. Two-Dimensional Object

THREE-DIMENSIONAL objects, such as cubes, can be measured in three dimensions (length, width, and height). Three-dimensional objects are also called **SOLIDS**, and the shape of a flattened solid is called a **NET**.

Figure 3.15. Three-Dimensional Object

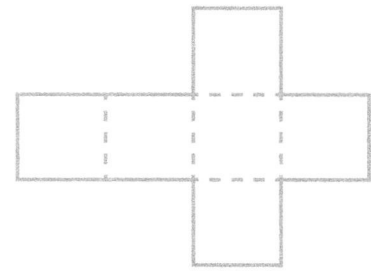

Figure 3.16. Net

EXAMPLE (MATHEMATICAL ACHIEVEMENT)

42. Angle *M* measures 36°. What is the measure of an angle supplementary to angle *M*?

EXAMPLE (QUANTITATIVE REASONING)

43. Which points and lines are contained in plane *M* in the figure below?

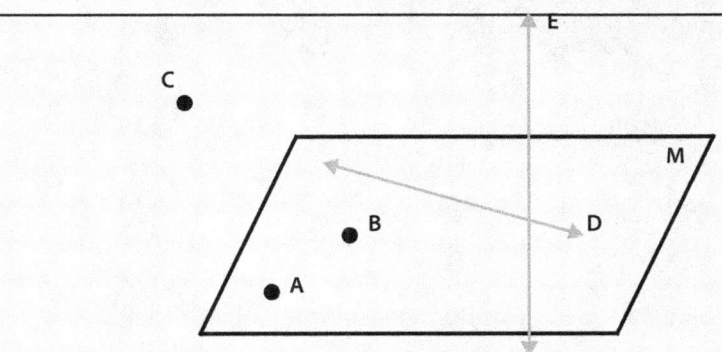

PERIMETER AND AREA

POLYGONS are two-dimensional shapes, such as triangles and squares, that have three or more straight sides. Regular polygons are polygons whose sides are all the same length.

Angles inside a polygon are **INTERIOR ANGLES**. Angles formed by one side of the polygon and a line extending outside the polygon are **EXTERIOR ANGLES**. The formulas below describe how to find interior and exterior angles of a regular polygon with side n.

TEACHING TIPS:
Don't worry about having students memorize these formulas—they'll be given on the test. Just make sure they understand all the terms.

▸ sum of interior angles = $(n - 2) \times 180°$

▸ measure of interior angle = $\frac{n-2}{n} \times 180°$

▸ sum of exterior angles = $360°$

▸ measure of exterior angle = $\frac{360°}{n}$

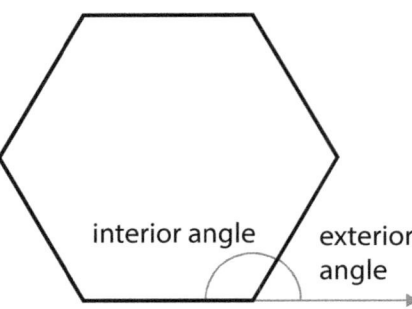

Figure 3.17. Interior and Exterior Angles

PERIMETER is the distance around a shape. It can be determined by adding the lengths of all sides of the shape. **AREA** is the amount of space a shape occupies. The area of an object is its length times its width and is measured in square units. For example, if a wall is 3 feet long and 2 feet wide, its area would be 6 square feet (ft²).

Table 3.8 gives the formulas for the area and perimeter of basic shapes. To find the area and perimeter of a circle, use the constant *pi* ($\pi = 3.14$).

TABLE 3.8. Area and Perimeter of Basic Shapes		
SHAPE	**AREAS**	**PERIMETER**
Triangle	$A = \frac{1}{2} bh$	$P = s_1 + s_2 + s_3$
Square	$A = s^2$	$P = 4s$
Rectangle	$A = l \times w$	$P = 2l + 2w$
Circle	$A = \pi r^2$	$C = 2\pi r$ (circumference)

An **EQUILATERAL** figure has sides that are all the same length. In an **EQUIANGULAR** figure, all the angles have the same measurement. To find the length of a side in an equilateral figure, divide the perimeter by the number of sides. To find the measure of each angle, divide the sum of all the interior angles by the number of angles.

EXAMPLE (MATHEMATICAL ACHIEVEMENT)

44. What is the perimeter of the regular polygon shown below?

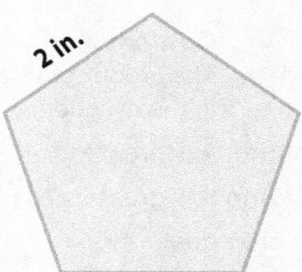

EXAMPLE (QUANTITATIVE REASONING)

45. **Column A**
The area of a square with a perimeter of 40 inches

Column B
The area of a rectangle with a perimeter of 50 inches

A) The quantity in Column A is greater.
B) The quantity in Column B is greater.
C) The two quantities are equal.
D) The relationship cannot be determined from the information given.

VOLUME AND SURFACE AREA

THREE-DIMENSIONAL SHAPES (also called **SOLIDS**) have depth in addition to width and length. **VOLUME** is expressed as the number of cubic units any solid can hold—that is, what it takes to fill it. **SURFACE AREA** is the sum of the areas of the two-dimensional figures that are found on its surface. Some three-dimensional shapes also have a unique property called a **SLANT HEIGHT (L)**, which is the distance from the base to the apex along a lateral face.

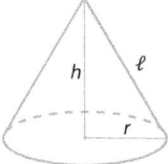

Figure 3.18. Slant Height in a Cone

TEACHING TIPS: Formulas for volume and surface area will be given on the exam.

EXAMPLE (MATHEMATICAL ACHIEVEMENT)

46. What is the surface area of a cube with a side length of 5 m?

EXAMPLE (QUANTITATIVE REASONING)

47. A cone and a cylinder cup both have the same diameter and same height. The volume of a cylinder is $V = \pi r^2 h$ and the volume of a cone is $V = \frac{1}{3}\pi r^2 h$.

Column A
The amount of water held in the cone

Column B
The amount of water held in the cylinder

A) The quantity in Column A is greater.

B) The quantity in Column B is greater.

C) The two quantities are equal.

D) The relationship cannot be determined from the information given.

SIMILARITY AND CONGRUENCE

When discussing shapes in geometry, the term **CONGRUENT** is used to mean that two shapes have the same shape and size (but not necessarily the same orientation or location). For example, if the length of two lines are equal, the two lines themselves are called congruent. Congruence is written using the symbol ≅. On figures, congruent parts are denoted with hash marks.

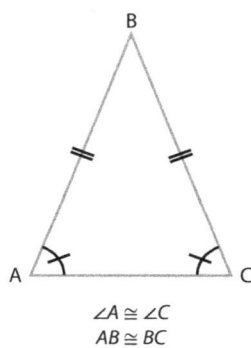

Figure 3.19. Congruent Parts of a Triangle

Shapes that are **SIMILAR** have the same shape but not the same size, meaning their corresponding angles are the same, but their lengths are not. For two shapes to be similar, the ratio of their corresponding sides must be a constant (usually written as k).

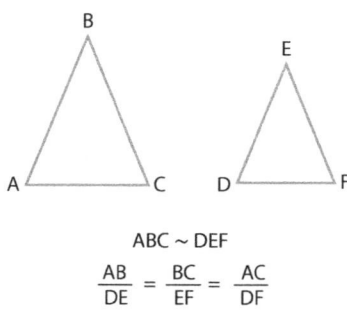

Figure 3.20. Similar Triangles

Similarity is described using the symbol ~.

EXAMPLE (MATHEMATICAL ACHIEVEMENT)

48. Squares *ABCD* and *MNOP* are similar. The side length of square *ABCD* is twice the side length of square *MNOP*. If the area of square *ABCD* is 100 mm², what is the area of square *MNOP*?

EXAMPLE (QUANTITATIVE REASONING)

49. Triangles *ABC* and *DFG* are similar.

Column A
The angle measure of BC

Column B
The angle measure of FG

- **A)** The quantity in Column A is greater.
- **B)** The quantity in Column B is greater.
- **C)** The two quantities are equal.
- **D)** The relationship cannot be determined from the information given.

Statistics

Statistics is the study of data. Analyzing data requires using **MEASURES OF CENTRAL TENDENCY** (mean, median, and mode) to identify trends or patterns.

The **MEAN** is the average; it is determined by adding all values and then dividing by the total number of values. For example, the average of the data set {16, 19, 19, 25, 27, 29, 75} is found by adding the values and dividing by 7.

$$\frac{16 + 19 + 19 + 25 + 27 + 29 + 75}{7} = \frac{210}{7} = 30$$

The **MEDIAN** is the number in the middle when the data set is arranged in order from least to greatest. For example, in the data set {16, 19, 19, 25, 27, 29, 75}, the median is 25. When a data set contains an even number of values, finding the median requires averaging the two middle values. In the data set {75, 80, 82, 100}, the two numbers in the middle are 80 and 82. Consequently, the median will be the average of these two values $\frac{80 + 82}{2} = 81$.

The **MODE** is the most frequent outcome in a data set. In the set {16, 19, 19, 25, 27, 29, 75}, the mode is 19 because it occurs twice, which is more than any of the other numbers. If several values appear an equally frequent number of times, both values are considered the mode. If every value in a data set appears only once, the data set has no mode.

TEACHING TIP:
Mode is most common. Median is in the middle (like a median in the road). Mean is average.

Other useful indicators include range and outliers. The **RANGE** is the difference between the highest and the lowest values in a data set. For example, the range of the set {16, 19, 19, 25, 27, 29, 75} is 75 − 16 = 59.

OUTLIERS, or data points that are much different from other data points, should be noted as they can skew the central tendency. In the data set {16, 19, 19, 25, 27, 29, 75}, the value 75 is far outside the other values and raises the value of the mean. Without the outlier, the mean is much closer to the other data points.

$$\frac{16 + 19 + 19 + 25 + 27 + 29 + 75}{7} = \frac{210}{7} = 30$$

$$\frac{16 + 19 + 19 + 25 + 27 + 29}{6} = \frac{135}{6} = 22.5$$

EXAMPLE (MATHEMATICAL ACHIEVEMENT)

50. In 2016, LeBron James scored 1954 points over 74 games. What was the mean number of points that he scored per game? (Round to the nearest tenth.)

EXAMPLE (QUANTITATIVE REASONING)

51. In his class, Bart surveyed his classmates to determine their favorite pizza topping. The data he found was as follows:

Anchovy	Pineapple
Olives	Olives
Pepperoni	Pineapple
Peppers	Bacon
Canadian Bacon	Pepperoni
Pepperoni	Pepperoni
Olives	Pepperoni
Pepperoni	Bacon
Pepperoni	Pepperoni
Olives	Pepperoni

Which topping represents the mode?

Probability

PROBABILITY describes how likely something is to happen. In probability, an **EVENT** is the single result of a trial, and an **OUTCOME** is a possible event that results from a trial. The collection of all possible outcomes for a particular trial is called the **SAMPLE SPACE**. For example, when rolling a die, the sample space is the numbers 1 – 6. Rolling a single number, such as 4, would be a single event.

COUNTING PRINCIPLES are methods used to find the number of possible outcomes for a given situation. The **FUNDAMENTAL COUNTING PRINCIPLE** states that, for a series of independent events, the number of outcomes can be found by multiplying the number of possible outcomes for each event. For example, if a die is rolled (6 possible outcomes) and a coin is tossed (2 possible outcomes), there are 6 × 2 = 12 total possible outcomes.

The probability of a single event occurring is the number of outcomes in which that event occurs (called favorable events) divided by the number of items in the sample space (total possible outcomes):

$$P \text{(an event)} = \frac{\text{number of favorable outcomes}}{\text{number of possible outsomes}}$$

The probability of any event occurring will always be a fraction or decimal between 0 and 1. A probability may also be expressed as a percent (e.g., a probability of 0.75 is 75%). An event with 0 probability will never occur, and an event with a probability of 1 is certain to occur. The probability of an event not occurring is referred to as that event's **COMPLEMENT**. The sum of an event's probability and the probability of that event's complement will always be 1.

To find the probability of multiple **INDEPENDENT EVENTS**—events whose outcomes do not affect each other—multiply the probability of each separate event. For example, the probability of getting the same number on a die during two consecutive rolls is

$$\frac{1}{6} \times \frac{1}{6} = \frac{1}{36}$$

EXAMPLE (MATHEMATICAL ACHIEVEMENT)

52. What is the probability that an even number results when a six-sided die is rolled?

EXAMPLE (MATHEMATICAL ACHIEVEMENT)

53. In a particular game, a person must draw a uniquely colored marble to win money. There are 12 blue marbles, 3 red marbles, and 1 yellow marble in a bag. If you draw a blue marble, then you lose your money; if you draw a red marble, you get your money back; if you draw a yellow marble, you win $5. What is the probability Marcia will not win $5?

ANSWER KEY

1. **1500 pencils.**

    Multiply the number of boxes by the number of pencils in each box to find the total number of pencils.

    $10 \times 150 =$ **1500 pencils**

2. **100**

    Use order of operations (PEMDAS) to solve the equation.

    First, complete the operations in the parentheses. Divide, then subtract.

    $8 \div 4 = 2$

    $12 - 2 = 10$

    Complete the exponents outside the parentheses.

    $10^2 =$ **100**

3. **−8°F**

    Because the temperature went down, add a negative number.

    $-3 + (-5) =$ **−8°F**

4. **C**

    The product of two negative numbers is positive.

    $-3 \times (-4) = 12$

    $3 \times 4 = 12$

    The two quantities are equal.

5. **$4\sqrt{3}$**

    Determine the largest square number that is a factor of the radicand, 48. Write the radicand as a product using that square number as a factor.

    $\sqrt{48} = \sqrt{16 \times 3} = \sqrt{16}\ \sqrt{3} =$ **$4\sqrt{3}$**

6. **D**

    Choose several values for x and substitute them into the expressions. Use values less than 0, between 0 and 1, and greater than 1.

    If $x = \frac{1}{4}$, Column A = $\frac{1}{2}$ and Column B = 0.63. Column B is greater.

    If $x = 64$, Column A = 8 and Column B = 4. Column A is greater.

    Therefore, it depends on the value of x to determine which quantity is greater. **The relationship cannot be determined from the information given.**

7. **4.27×10^3**

    To add, the powers of 10 must be the same. Convert the first value so the power of 10 is 2.

    $3.8 \times 10^3 = 3.8 \times 10 \times 10^2 = 38 \times 10^2$

    Add the terms together and write the answer in proper scientific notation.

    $(38 \times 10^2) + (4.7 \times 10^2) = (38 + 4.7) \times 10^2 = 42.7 \times 10^2 =$ **4.27×10^3**

8. **B**

   Convert each value to decimal notation.
   Column A: $3.8 \times 10^{-3} = 0.0038$
   Column B: $1.2 \times 10^{-2} = 0.012$
   Since $0.012 > 0.0038$, **the quantity in Column B is greater.**

9. **4**

   $-(3)^2 + 4(5) + (5 - 6)^2 - 8$
   $= -(3)^2 + 4(5) + (-1)^2 - 8$
   $= -9 + 4(5) + 1 - 8$
   $= -9 + 20 + 1 - 8$
   $= 11 + 1 - 8$
   $= 12 - 8$
   $= \mathbf{4}$

10. **B**

    Use the order of operations to simplify each expression.
    Column A: Simplify the expression in the parentheses, $2 \times 3 = 6$. Solve by subtracting, $6 - 6 = 0$.
    Column B: Simplify the parentheses, $6 - 2 = 4$. Solve by multiplying, $4 \times 3 = 12$.
    $0 < 12$; **the quantity in Column B is greater.**

11. $\frac{7}{12}$ **pizza**

    The common denominator is $4 \times 3 = 12$.
    Convert each fraction to the common denominator.
    $\frac{1}{4}\left(\frac{3}{3}\right) = \frac{3}{12}$
    $\frac{1}{3}\left(\frac{4}{4}\right) = \frac{4}{12}$
    Add the numerators and keep the denominator the same.
    $\frac{3}{12} + \frac{4}{12} = \frac{7}{12}$
    Together, they have $\frac{7}{12}$ of a pizza.

12. **C**

    Write the value in Column B as a mixed number.
    Divide the numerator and denominator by 2 to get $\frac{19}{4}$.
    Convert $\frac{19}{4}$ to a mixed number, $\frac{19}{4} = 4\frac{3}{4}$.
    The two quantities are equal.

13. **$38.74**

    Rewrite the numbers vertically, lining up the decimal points.
    Add:

    ```
        2.20
       32.54
    +   4.00
       38.74
    ```
    The total bill was **$38.74**.

Mathematics

14. D

It can be inferred that George has at least 4 pennies because he has $7.24 in pocket change. Possibly George has 794 pennies, 72 dimes and 4 pennies, or some other combination. There is no information given regarding the number of pennies, nickels, dimes, quarters, half dollars, and any other denomination of change he has. **The relationship cannot be determined from the information given.**

15. 1200 mg

Write a proportion using x for the missing value.

$$\frac{60 \text{ kg}}{90 \text{ mg}} = \frac{80 \text{ kg}}{x \text{ mg}}$$

Cross multiply.

$60(x) = 80(90)$

$60x = 7200$

Divide by 60.

$x = 1200$

The proper dosage is **1200 mg**.

16. 625 students

Convert the percentage to a decimal.

$40\% = 0.4$

Write the proportion.

$$\frac{250}{x} = \frac{0.4}{1}$$

Cross multiply.

$250(1) = 0.4(x)$

$250 = 0.4x$

Divide both sides by 0.4.

$625 = x$

There are **625 students** in Jacob's class.

17. 20 appointments

Set up a proportion and solve.

$$\frac{\text{part}}{\text{whole}} = \frac{\%}{100}$$

$$\frac{16}{x} = \frac{80}{100}$$

$16(100) = 80(x)$

$\boldsymbol{x = 20}$

18. $825

Identify the known values, then substitute in the percentage equation.

original amount = $1500

percent change = 45% = 0.45

amount of change = ?

amount of change = original amount × percent change → $1500 × 0.45 = $675

original price − amount of change = new price

$1500 − $675 = **$825**

19. **171 invitations**

    Kevin can only have 120 people attend. More than 120 people can be invited if he expects 30% to decline his invitation.

    Convert percentage to decimal.

    Accept invitation → 70% = 0.7

    Let x = the number of people he can invite.

    $x(0.7) = 120$

    $x = \frac{120}{0.7}$

    $x =$ **171**

20. **12,500 registered voters**

    Hank earned 40% or 4000 of the vote.

    Write and solve the proportion.

    $\frac{4{,}000}{x} = \frac{40}{100} \to x = 10{,}000$

    If voter turnout was 80%, then the number of registered voters is equivalent to:

    $\frac{10{,}000}{x} = \frac{80}{100} \to x =$ **12,500**

21. **52,000**

    Round each town population to the nearest thousand.

    1<u>2</u>,341 ≈ 12,000

    <u>8</u>975 ≈ 9000

    <u>9</u>431 ≈ 9000

    1<u>0</u>,521 ≈ 11,000

    1<u>1</u>,427 ≈ 11,000

    Add to find the total population.

    12,000 + 9000 + 9000 + 11,000 + 11,000 = **52,000**

22. $\begin{bmatrix} \mathbf{9} & \mathbf{-4} & \mathbf{6} \\ \mathbf{-7} & \mathbf{3} & \mathbf{9} \end{bmatrix}$

    Add the corresponding elements in each matrix.

    $\begin{bmatrix} 7 & 4 & 1 \\ -6 & 3 & 5 \end{bmatrix} + \begin{bmatrix} 2 & -8 & 5 \\ -1 & 0 & 4 \end{bmatrix}$

    $= \begin{bmatrix} 7+2 & 4+(-8) & 1+5 \\ -6+(-1) & 3+0 & 5+4 \end{bmatrix}$

    $= \begin{bmatrix} \mathbf{9} & \mathbf{-4} & \mathbf{6} \\ \mathbf{-7} & \mathbf{3} & \mathbf{9} \end{bmatrix}$

23. $\begin{bmatrix} 12 & -6 \\ 8 & 20 \end{bmatrix}$

Multiple each term in the matrix by the scalar 2.

$2\begin{bmatrix} 6 & -3 \\ 4 & 10 \end{bmatrix}$

$= \begin{bmatrix} 2 \times 6 & 2 \times -3 \\ 2 \times 4 & 2 \times 10 \end{bmatrix}$

$= \begin{bmatrix} 12 & -6 \\ 8 & 20 \end{bmatrix}$

24. **1140**

The order of the items doesn't matter. Use the formula for combinations:

$C(n, r) = \frac{n!}{(n-r)!r!}$

$C(20, 3) = \frac{20!}{(20!/(20-3)!)3!} = \frac{20!}{17!3!} = \frac{(20)(19)(18)}{3!} = $ **1140**

25. **720**

To find the number of unique permutations of five letters in *pickle*, use the permutation formula:

$P(n, r) = \frac{n!}{(n-r)!}$

$P(6, 5) = \frac{6!}{(6-5)!} = \frac{720}{1} = $ **720**

26. **28**

Find the common difference by subtracting two consecutive terms.

$-40 - (-57) = 17$

Substituting in the formula:

$a_n = a_1 + (n-1)d$

$a_6 = -57 + (6-1)17$

$a_6 = $ **28**

27. **B**

In the arithmetic sequence, each value will increase by 6.

2, 8, 14, . . .

In the geometric sequence, each value will increase by a multiple of 6.

2, 12, 72, . . .

The values in the geometric sequence increase more rapidly, so the 100th value of the geometric sequence will be larger than the 100th value of the arithmetic sequence. **The quantity in Column B is greater**.

28. **59**

Substitute the value −10 for *a* in the expression and simply.

$\frac{a^2}{4} - 3a + 4$

$= \frac{(-10)^2}{4} - 3(-10) + 4$

$= \frac{100}{4} + 30 + 4$

$= 25 + 30 + 4 = \mathbf{59}$

29. $\mathbf{2xy + 3x^2}$

    Substitute the given terms for *a* and *b*.
    $2a + 3b$
    $= 2(xy) + 3(x^2)$
    $= \mathbf{2xy + 3x^2}$

30. $\mathbf{6x - 10y + 2z}$

    Combine like terms.
    $4x - 3y + 12z + 2x - 7y - 10z$
    $= (4x + 2x) + (-3y - 7y) + (12z - 10z)$
    $= \mathbf{6x - 10y + 2z}$

31. $\mathbf{9g + 10r}$

    Write an expression for each person's tickets and then combine like terms.
    Paul = 3 boxes of green tickets and 8 boxes of red tickets: $3g + 8r$.
    Paula = 6 boxes of green tickets and 2 boxes of red tickets: $6g + 2r$.
    Combining like terms gives $\mathbf{9g + 10r}$.

32. $\mathbf{5x^3 - 10xc + 50x}$

    Distribute the term $5x$ by multiplying by each of the three terms inside the parentheses:
    $5x(x^2 - 2c + 10)$
    $(5x)(x^2) = 5x^3$
    $(5x)(-2c) = -10xc$
    $(5x)(10) = 50x$
    $5x(x^2 - 2c + 10) = \mathbf{5x^3 - 10xc + 50x}$

33. **C**

    Simplify each expression.
    In Column A, combine like terms: $4x + 2x = 6x$. The simplified expression for Column A is $6x - 2y - 10$.
    In Column B, distribute the 2 into $3x - y - 5$, giving $6x - 2y - 10$. **The two quantities are equal.**

34. **8**

    Distribute the 5 and combine like terms:
    $5(x + 3) - 12 = 43$
    $5x + 15 - 12 = 43$
    $5x + 3 = 43$
    Subtract 3 from both sides:
    $5x + 3 - 3 = 43 - 3$
    $5x = 40$

Divide both sides by 5:
$\frac{5x}{5} = \frac{40}{5}$
$x = 8$

35. **$85**

    Determine the amount per hour Mandy will charge this family.

    Charges: $8 for one child plus $3 each for additional children.

    4 children → 8 + 3 × 3 = $17 per hour.

    If she babysits for 5 hours, then she should expect to earn 17 × 5 = **$85**.

36. **x > 12**

    Inequalities can be solved just like equations.

    $4x + 10 > 58$

    Subtract 10 from both sides:

    $4x + 10 - 10 > 58 - 10$

    $4x > 48$

    Divide by 4 to isolate x:

    $\frac{4x}{54} > \frac{48}{4} \quad \frac{4x}{54}$

    x > 12

37. **12t + 15p + 45s < 2500**

    The team must spend less than $2500 on uniforms, so this problem is an inequality.

    Identify the quantities:

    number of shirts = t

    total cost of shirts = $12t$

    number of pants = p

    total cost of pants = $15p$

    number of pairs of shoes = s

    total cost of shoes = $45s$

    The cost of all the items must be less than $2500: **12t + 15p + 45s < 2500**.

38. **3**

    $6x - 2y - 8 = 0$

    Write in slope-intercept form (solve for y).

    $\frac{-2y}{-2} = \frac{-6x}{-2} + \frac{8}{-2} \quad \frac{-6x}{-2}$

    $y = 3x - 4$

    The slope is the coefficient of x, which is **3**.

39. **II**

    Starting at the origin, move 5 units to the left and then up 2 units. The point is located in the top left quadrant, which is **quadrant II**.

40. **250 cm**

Use a conversion factor to convert centimeters to meters.

2.5 m × $\frac{100 \text{ cm}}{1 \text{m}}$ = $\frac{2.5 \times 100 \text{ cm}}{1 \text{m}}$ = **250 cm**

41. **C**

    Compare 3 kilometers and 300 dekameters. Convert both amounts to meters.
    Column A: Multiply 3 by 1000 (1000 m = 1 km) to get 3000 meters.
    Column B: Multiply 300 by 10 to get 3000 meters. **The two quantities are equal.**

42. **144°**

    Supplementary angles have a sum of 180°. Subtract the measure of angle M from 180°.
    180° − 36° = **144°**

43. **$\dot{A}$, $\dot{B}$, $\overleftrightarrow{D}$**

    Points A and B and line D all lie on plane M.

44. **10 in**

    Add the lengths of all the sides.
    2 in + 2 in + 2 in + 2 in + 2 in = **10 in**

45. **D**

    Column A: Square → P = 40 inches, then it must have side lengths of 10 inches.
    Area = 10 × 10 or 100 in²
    Column B: Rectangle → P = 50 inches.
    There is more than one rectangle that can satisfy a perimeter of 50 inches. A few examples are:
    Length = 24 in and width = 1 in → area = 24 in²
    Length = 12 in and width = 13 in → area = 156 in²
    Length = 6 in and width = 19 in → area = 114 in²
    There are some values that make the area of the rectangle smaller than the square or larger than the square. **The relationship cannot be determined from the information given.**

46. **150 m²**

    A cube has six faces, each of which is a square.
    Find the area of each side using the formula for the area of a square:
    $A = s^2 = 5^2 = 25$ m²
    Multiply the area by 6 (because the cube has six faces):
    $SA = 25(6) =$ **150 m²**

47. **B**

    Volume of a cylinder: $V = \pi r^2 h$
    Volume of a cone: $V = \frac{1}{3} \pi r^2 h$

If the cone and cylinder both have the same diameter, they have the same radius. It is given that they are the same height. The cone would hold $\frac{1}{3}$ less water than the cylinder. **The quantity in Column B is greater.**

48. 25 mm²

Find the length of a side in square ABCD using the formula for the area of a square.

$A = s^2 = 100$ mm²

$s = 10$ mm

The side length of square MNOP is $\frac{1}{2}$ the side length of square ABCD.

10 mm ÷ 2 = 5 mm

Find the area of square MNOP using the formula for the area of a square.

$A = s^2 = 5^2 =$ **25 mm²**

49. C

Similar figures will always have the same angle measurement but may have different lengths. All corresponding angles are congruent and side lengths are proportional. **The two quantities are equal.**

50. 26.4 points

The mean is the average number of points per game. Divide the total number of points by the number of games played:

$\frac{1954}{74} \approx$ **26.4**

51. Pepperoni

Anchovy	1
Pineapple	2
Olives	4
Pepperoni	9
Bacon	2
Canadian Bacon	1

The mode occurs the most often. The mode is **Pepperoni**.

52. $\frac{1}{2}$

$P(\text{rolling even}) = \frac{\text{number of favorable outcomes}}{\text{total number of possible outcomes}} = \frac{3}{6} = \frac{1}{2}$

53. $\frac{15}{16}$

Win \$5 = yellow marble

There are 16 possible marbles and only 1 yellow marble.

The probability of drawing a yellow marble = $\frac{1}{16}$.

The probability she would not win = $1 - \frac{1}{16} = \frac{15}{16}$.

CHAPTER FOUR
The Essay

You will be asked to write a short essay on the ISEE. Schools use the essay as a way to get to know you better as a person and to get an idea of your writing skills.

You will be given a prompt with a topic. Expect to write about a topic you have already thought about, like whether students should wear uniforms to school, be allowed to have their phones in class, or have restrictions on social media. You have thirty minutes to write your essay.

In a strong essay, you will clearly state your feelings on the topic, offer specific ideas and examples that support your position, and stay organized. A good essay also includes strong vocabulary and varied sentence structure. The following sections walk through these steps and provide examples.

Writing a Thesis Statement

The thesis, or **THESIS STATEMENT**, is a sentence that sums up the main idea of an essay. It presents your point of view on an issue. In other words, it tells readers specifically what you think and what you will discuss.

Writing a good thesis statement is as simple as stating your idea and why you think it's true or correct.

> **EXAMPLE**
>
> *Take a position on the following topic in your essay. You can choose to write about either of the two viewpoints discussed in the prompt, or you may argue for a third point of view.*
>
> Many high schools have begun to adopt 1:1 technology programs, meaning that each school provides every student with a device such as a laptop or tablet. Teachers who support these initiatives say that the

technology improves the classroom experience and that students need to learn technology skills. On the other hand, opponents worry about distractions and dangers like cyber-bullying or unsupervised internet use as reasons not to provide students with such devices.

Possible thesis statements:

Providing technology to every student is good for education because it allows students to learn important skills such as typing, web design, and video editing; it also gives students more opportunities to work cooperatively with their classmates and teachers.

I disagree with the idea that schools should provide technology to students because most students will simply be distracted by games and websites when they should be studying or doing homework.

Schools have a responsibility to teach students how to use technology safely; providing each student with a laptop or tablet is one way to help them do that.

Structuring the Essay

There are a few different ways to organize an essay, but some basics apply no matter what the style.

Essays may differ in how they present an idea, but they all have the same basic parts—introduction, body, and conclusion. The most common essay types are persuasive essays and expository essays.

A **PERSUASIVE** essay takes a position on an issue and attempts to show the reader why it's correct. An **EXPOSITORY** essay explains different aspects of an issue without necessarily taking a side.

INTRODUCTIONS

Present your argument or idea in the introduction. Usually, the introduction is a paragraph that ends with the thesis statement. It clearly sets forth the position or point the essay will prove. The introduction is a good place to bring up complexities, counterarguments, and context, all of which will help the reader understand the reasoning behind your position on the issue at hand. Later, revisit those issues and wrap all of them up in the conclusion.

> **EXAMPLE**
>
> Below is an example of an introduction. Note that it provides some context for the argument, acknowledges an opposing perspective, and gives the reader a good idea of the issue's complexities. Pay attention to the thesis statement in the last few lines, which clearly states the author's position.

Technology has changed massively in recent years, but today's generation barely notices—high school students are already experienced with the internet, computers, apps, cameras, cell phones, and more. Teenagers must learn to use these tools safely and responsibly. Opponents of 1:1 technology programs might argue that students will be distracted or misuse the technology, but that is exactly why schools must teach them to use it. By providing technology to students, schools can help them apply it positively by creating great projects with other students, communicating with teachers and classmates, and doing research for class projects. Schools have a responsibility to teach students how to use technology safely; providing each student with a laptop or tablet is one way to help them do that.

THE BODY PARAGRAPHS

The body of an essay consists of a series of structured paragraphs. You may write paragraphs that describe or explain each reason you give in your thesis. Or you could address the issue as a problem and offer a solution in a separate paragraph. You could even tell a story that demonstrates your point (make sure to break it into paragraphs around related ideas). Finally, you might compare and contrast the merits of two opposing sides of the issue (make sure to draw a conclusion about which is better at the end).

Make sure that each paragraph is well organized, beginning with a topic sentence to introduce the main idea, followed by supporting ideas and examples. No extra ideas unrelated to the paragraph's focus should appear. Use transition words and phrases to connect body paragraphs, and improve the flow and readability of your essay.

In the following section (Providing Supporting Evidence), you will find an example of a paragraph that is internally consistent and explains one of the main reasons given in one of the sample thesis statements above. Your essay should have one or more paragraphs like this to form the main body.

CONCLUSIONS

To end your essay, write a conclusion that reminds the reader why you were talking about these topics in the first place. Go back to the ideas in the introduction and thesis statement, but be careful not to simply restate your ideas; rather, remind the reader of your point of view.

EXAMPLE

Here is a sample conclusion paragraph that could go with the introduction above. Notice that this conclusion talks about the same topics as the introduction (changing technology and the responsibility of schools), but it does not simply rewrite the thesis.

As technology continues to change, teens will need to adapt to it. Schools already teach young people academic and life skills, so it makes sense that they would teach students how to use technology appropriately, too. Providing students with their own devices is one part of that important task, and schools should be supported in it.

Providing Supporting Evidence

In your essay, you should provide specific evidence supporting your point of view. Whenever you make a general statement, follow it with specific examples to convince the reader that you are right. These specific examples do not bring new ideas to the paragraph. Instead, they explain or defend the general ideas that have already been stated.

The following are some examples of general statements and specific statements that provide more detailed support:

GENERAL: Students may get distracted online or access harmful websites.

SPECIFIC: Some students spend too much time using chat features, social media, or online games. Others spend time reading websites that have nothing to do with an assignment.

SPECIFIC: Teens often think they are hidden behind their computer screens. If teenagers give out personal information such as age or location on a website, it can lead to dangerous strangers seeking them out.

GENERAL: Schools can teach students how to use technology appropriately and offer them new tools.

SPECIFIC: Schools can help students learn to use technology to work on class projects, communicate with classmates and teachers, and carry out research for classwork.

SPECIFIC: Providing students with laptops or tablets will allow them to get lots of practice using technology and programs at home, and only school districts can ensure that these tools are distributed widely, especially to students who may not have them at home.

> **EXAMPLE**
>
> *The following is an example of a structured paragraph that uses specific supporting ideas. This paragraph supports the thesis introduced above (see Introductions).*
>
> Providing students with their own laptop or tablet will allow them to explore new programs and software in class with teachers and classmates and to practice using it at home. In schools without laptops for students, classes have to visit computer labs where they share old computers often missing keys or that run so slowly they are hardly powered on before class ends. When a teacher tries to show students how to use a new tool

> or website, students must scramble to follow along and have no time to explore the new feature. If they can take laptops home instead, students can do things like practice editing video clips or photographs until they are perfect. They can email classmates or use shared files to collaborate even after school. If schools expect students to learn these skills, it is the schools' responsibility to provide students with enough opportunities to practice them.
>
> This paragraph has some general statements:
>
> *... their own laptop or tablet will allow them to explore new programs and software... and to practice...*
>
> *...it is the schools' responsibility to provide... enough opportunities...*
>
> It also has some specific examples to back them up:
>
> *...computers... run so slowly they are hardly powered on... students must scramble to follow along and have no time to explore...*
>
> *They can email classmates or use shared files to collaborate...*

Writing Well

Paying attention to these details will make your perspective clear and help readers understand your writing.

TRANSITIONS

Transitions are words, phrases, and ideas that help connect ideas throughout a text. You should use them between sentences and between paragraphs. Some common transitions include *then, next, in other words, as well,* and *in addition to*. Be creative with your transitions, and make sure you understand what the transition you are using shows about the relationship between the ideas. For instance, the transition *although* implies that there is some contradiction between the first idea and the second.

SYNTAX

The way you write sentences is important to maintaining the reader's interest. Try to begin sentences differently. Make some sentences long and some sentences short. Write simple sentences. Write complex sentences that have complex ideas in them. Readers appreciate variety.

There are four basic types of sentences: simple, compound, complex, and compound-complex. Try to use some of each type. Be sure that your sentences make sense, though—it's better to have clear and simple writing that a reader can understand than to have complex, confusing syntax that does not clearly express the idea.

WORD CHOICE AND TONE

The words you choose influence the impression you make on readers. Use words that are specific, direct, and appropriate to the task. For instance, a formal text may benefit from complex sentences and impressive vocabulary, while it may be more appropriate to use simple vocabulary and sentences in writing intended for a young audience.

Use strong vocabulary; avoid using vague, general words such as *good*, *bad*, *very*, or *a lot* if you can think of a better way to express yourself. However, make sure that you are comfortable with the vocabulary you choose; if you are unsure about the word's meaning or its use in the context of your essay, don't use it at all.

EDITING, REVISING, AND PROOFREADING

Your essay will be timed, so you will not have very much time for these steps. Spend any time you have left after writing the essay looking over it and checking for spelling and grammar mistakes that may interfere with a reader's understanding.

Common mistakes to look out for include: subject/verb disagreement, pronoun/antecedent disagreement, comma splices and run-ons, and sentence fragments (phrases or dependent clauses unconnected to an independent clause).

CHAPTER FIVE
Practice Test One

Verbal Reasoning
SYNONYMS

Directions: Find the synonym or the word closest in meaning.

1. AMALGAM
   A) blend
   B) process
   C) schedule
   D) conference

2. SUCCUMB
   A) ignore
   B) fight
   C) surrender
   D) enjoy

3. POTENT
   A) powerful
   B) weak
   C) detrimental
   D) nutritional

4. PRONE
   A) excited
   B) flat
   C) unconscious
   D) uncomfortable

5. AMBULATORY
   A) healthy
   B) recovered
   C) symptomatic
   D) walking

6. SUPERFICIAL
   A) shallow
   B) impressive
   C) gruesome
   D) jagged

7. REGRESS
   A) get better
   B) strengthen
   C) worsen
   D) fail

8. RESPIRATION
   A) breathing
   B) sleeping
   C) digestion
   D) heartbeat

9. PRAGMATIC
   A) practical
   B) logical
   C) emotional
   D) aloof

10. RETAIN
    A) forget
    B) shed
    C) filter
    D) hold

11. DYSFUNCTIONAL
    A) vast
    B) expensive
    C) intricate
    D) flawed

12. ACCOUNTABILITY
    A) responsibility
    B) accuracy
    C) compliance
    D) confidence

13. DIMINISH
    A) identify
    B) decrease
    C) stop
    D) intensify

14. BENIGN
    A) problematic
    B) worrisome
    C) harmless
    D) unattractive

15. ABSTAIN
    A) ingest
    B) resist
    C) refrain
    D) intake

16. VITAL
    A) contrary
    B) necessary
    C) unrelated
    D) secondary

17. ADHERE
    A) follow
    B) reject
    C) uphold
    D) interpret

18. COHORT
    A) university
    B) acquaintance
    C) group
    D) associate

19. DELETERIOUS
    A) helpful
    B) harmful
    C) gentle
    D) constructive

20. MALAISE
    A) nausea
    B) headache
    C) unease
    D) vomiting

SINGLE-WORD RESPONSE

Directions: Choose the word that best completes the sentence.

1. Because he acted so _____, his friends thought he didn't care about them, so they stopped hanging around with him.
    A) snobbish
    B) inconsequential
    C) skittish
    D) nonchalant

2. The principal was a _____ leader; she showed kindness to all students and staff.
   A) benevolent
   B) tyrannical
   C) laudable
   D) pugnacious

3. The young children teased the boy _____, causing him to cry and leave the party.
   A) benevolently
   B) furiously
   C) maliciously
   D) innocently

4. Jack's friends _____ him after he made an offensive comment in class; they ignored his calls and invitations to a party.
   A) snubbed
   B) invoked
   C) regarded
   D) encouraged

5. Don't be such a _____! Practice what you preach.
   A) traitor
   B) hypocrite
   C) comedian
   D) humanitarian

6. The veterinarian faced a _____; she needed to operate on the wounded animal, but the animal wasn't in stable condition and might not make it through surgery.
   A) opportunity
   B) chance
   C) dilemma
   D) disagreement

7. Competing in the Olympics is quite _____; athletes try their hardest, often pushing their muscles and their minds to the limit.
   A) half-hearted
   B) light
   C) fabulous
   D) strenuous

8. Do not _____ over things you cannot control. There are plenty of other things to agonize over.
   A) fret
   B) gloss
   C) disappear
   D) soothe

9. This plant is very _____; it survived through the winter and is now flourishing!
   A) direct
   B) feeble
   C) anemic
   D) robust

10. The soldiers made a _____ effort throughout the war; their courage and bravery should be rewarded.
    A) diligent
    B) steadfast
    C) valiant
    D) mild

CONTINUE

11. The teacher asked Paige to _____ the discussion; she was shy at first, but then she began to ask questions.

   A) table
   B) stop
   C) initiate
   D) withhold from

12. The lively, _____ students were wide awake at the beginning of the day. After lunch, however, they became lifeless.

   A) animated
   B) studious
   C) disappointed
   D) bewildered

13. The principal _____ the students who were sent to his office for punishment.

   A) stirred
   B) energized
   C) admonished
   D) condescended

14. The two skaters were very _____ and skated well together, working through difficult maneuvers with ease.

   A) likeable
   B) charming
   C) compatible
   D) different

15. The _____ waitress made the patrons feel welcomed and at home in the restaurant.

   A) spiteful
   B) incompatible
   C) consistent
   D) amiable

DOUBLE-WORD RESPONSE

Directions: Choose the pair of words that best completes the sentence.

1. My guilt was _____ after I found out that I wasn't to blame for the _____ accident.

   A) wasted... devastating
   B) ravaged... harmful
   C) engorged... distressing
   D) assuaged... dreadful

2. The author wrote a _____ sequel; it was completely _____ and no one liked it.

   A) trite... lackluster
   B) banal... inspiring
   C) predictable... original
   D) facile... remarkable

3. The bodybuilder had muscles that were _____ and _____; he won every weight-lifting contest in the country.

   A) strong... feeble
   B) sinewy... brawny
   C) frail... lean
   D) anemic... robust

4. Because of the babysitter's reputation for being _____, kids from the neighborhood begged their parents to find someone new to watch them; they didn't want to _____ over their bedtime.

A) mischievous... debate
B) intellectual... diverge
C) stoic... clash
D) argumentative... squabble

5. After the mountain bike accident, we tried to _____ the bicycle, but we soon realized it was _____ because it would cost more to repair it than it would to buy a new one.

A) fix... viable
B) save... easy
C) salvage... impractical
D) abandon... effortless

Answer Key

SYNONYMS

1. **A)** Amalgam means a mixture or blend.

2. **C)** Succumb means to yield or stop resisting.

3. **A)** Potent means powerful, strong, or effective.

4. **B)** Prone means someone or something is lying flat.

5. **D)** Ambulatory means able to walk.

6. **A)** Superficial means shallow (often in character or attitude) or on the surface.

7. **C)** Regress means to move backward, often to a worse state.

8. **A)** Respiration means breathing.

9. **A)** Pragmatic means concerned with practical matters and results.

10. **D)** Retain means to hold or keep in possession.

11. **D)** Dysfunctional means not functioning properly.

12. **A)** Accountability means to be responsible for something or to be held to account.

13. **B)** Diminish means to become less in amount or intensity.

14. **C)** Benign means not harmful.

15. **C)** Abstain means to choose to avoid or not participate; to refrain.

16. **B)** Vital means essential to existence or well-being.

17. **A)** Adhere means to hold closely to an idea or course or to follow devotedly.

18. **C)** Cohort describes a group of people with something in common.

19. **B)** Deleterious means harmful or deadly to living things.

20. **C)** Malaise means a general feeling of illness and discomfort.

SINGLE-WORD RESPONSE

1. **D)** Nonchalant means to be without a care in the world and is the best response. The context clue "he didn't care about them" tells us that he is nonchalant.

2. **A)** Benevolent means kind, so the context clue "kindness" in the second part of the sentence directs us to this answer.

3. **C)** Maliciously means unkindly or cruelly. Since the children teased the boy so much that he cried and left the party, then the teasing must have been extremely unkind or cruel.

4. **A)** To snub someone is to ignore them.

5. **B)** A hypocrite is someone who does the opposite of what he or she says.

6. **C)** A dilemma is a difficult choice.

7. **D)** Strenuous means determined, vigorous, and demanding.

8. **A)** To fret is to worry or agonize over.

9. **D)** The plant is robust: it is sturdy and strong.

10. **C)** Valiant means brave.

11. **C)** Because Paige began to speak, she initiated or started the discussion.

12. **A)** The key context clues are "wide awake" and "lively," which are synonyms for animated.

13. **C)** The principal would scold or admonish students who are in trouble.

14. **C)** The two skaters worked well together because they were compatible, which means well-matched.

15. **D)** Amiable means likable or friendly.

DOUBLE-WORD RESPONSE

1. **D)** Assuaged means diminished, alleviated, or eased. Dreadful means awful or horrible.

2. **A)** Trite means commonplace or unoriginal, and lackluster means boring or uninteresting.

3. **B)** Sinewy and brawny are synonyms indicating strength.

4. **D)** Argumentative means pugnacious or eager to argue; to squabble means to bicker or disagree.

5. **C)** To salvage is to repair or fix; impractical means unreasonable or unrealistic.

Quantitative Reasoning

1.

Column A	Column B
The sum of the angles in an acute triangle	The sum of the angles in a right triangle

- A) The quantity in Column A is greater.
- B) The quantity in Column B is greater.
- C) The two quantities are equal.
- D) The relationship cannot be determined from the information given.

2.

Column A	Column B
The y-intercept of the line $y = 4x$	The slope of the line $y = 4$

- A) The quantity in Column A is greater.
- B) The quantity in Column B is greater.
- C) The two quantities are equal.
- D) The relationship cannot be determined from the information given.

3.

Column A	Column B
The number of unique ways we can arrange the letters in the word MATH	The number of unique ways we can arrange the letters in the word FIRE

- A) The quantity in Column A is greater.
- B) The quantity in Column B is greater.
- C) The two quantities are equal.
- D) The relationship cannot be determined from the information given.

4.

Column A	Column B
30% of 50	50% of 30

- A) The quantity in Column A is greater.
- B) The quantity in Column B is greater.
- C) The two quantities are equal.
- D) The relationship cannot be determined from the information given.

5. For $0 < x < 1$

Column A	Column B
x^2	x^4

- A) The quantity in Column A is greater.
- B) The quantity in Column B is greater.
- C) The two quantities are equal.
- D) The relationship cannot be determined from the information given.

6.

Column A	Column B
The slope of the line $y = -x - 2$	The slope of a line perpendicular to $y = -x - 2$

- A) The quantity in Column A is greater.
- B) The quantity in Column B is greater.
- C) The two quantities are equal.
- D) The relationship cannot be determined from the information given.

7. Given $a > b$)

Column A	Column B
$3a$	$4b$

- A) The quantity in Column A is greater.
- B) The quantity in Column B is greater.
- C) The two quantities are equal.
- D) The relationship cannot be determined from the information given.

8. Mr. Harkins receives the AP test scores from his AP Microeconomics class. His scores are: 1, 2, 2, 2, 3, 3, 3, 3, 3, 3, 4, 4, 4, 5, 5.

Column A	Column B
The median test score	The mode test score

- A) The quantity in Column A is greater.
- B) The quantity in Column B is greater.
- C) The two quantities are equal.
- D) The relationship cannot be determined from the information given.

9. Triangles *ABC* and *DFG* are congruent.

Column A	Column B
The area of Triangle *ABC*	The area of Triangle *DFG*

- A) The quantity in Column A is greater.
- B) The quantity in Column B is greater.
- C) The two quantities are equal.
- D) The relationship cannot be determined from the information given.

10. The mean score of a test is 78, the median is 83, the mode is 80, and the range is 37. Ms. Robinson later curves the tests by adding 5 points to each test, and John's new score is 87.

Column A	Column B
John's new test score	The new median test score

- **A)** The quantity in Column A is greater.
- **B)** The quantity in Column B is greater.
- **C)** The two quantities are equal.
- **D)** The relationship cannot be determined from the information given.

11. Given $x \nabla y = 3x - y$,

Column A	Column B
$2 \nabla 3$	$3 \nabla 2$

- **A)** The quantity in Column A is greater.
- **B)** The quantity in Column B is greater.
- **C)** The two quantities are equal.
- **D)** The relationship cannot be determined from the information given.

12. If the following expression is written in the form 10^n, what is the value of n?

$$\frac{(10^2)^3}{(10^{-2})^2}$$

- **A)** 2
- **B)** 5
- **C)** 6
- **D)** 10

13. Mr. Smith gives a science test and finds the mean of his class's scores is 78, the median is 74, the mode is 77, and the range is 24. He decides to curve his tests by adding 7 points to each of the test scores. Which of the following values will remain the same after he curves the scores?

- **A)** mean
- **B)** median
- **C)** mode
- **D)** range

14. Which of the following statements is true for the line $x = 3$?

- **A)** It has a slope of 3.
- **B)** It has a y-intercept of 3.
- **C)** It does not have an x-intercept.
- **D)** It has an undefined slope.

15. Which expression is equivalent to dividing 400 by 16?

- **A)** $2(200 - 8)$
- **B)** $(400 \div 4) \div 12$
- **C)** $(216 \div 8) + (184 \div 8)$
- **D)** $(216 \div 16) + (184 \div 16)$

16. A recipe calls for $2\frac{1}{4}$ cups of flour. Which of the following measurement tools can be used to measure the flour?

- **A.** $\frac{1}{4}$ cup
- **B.** $\frac{1}{3}$ cup
- **C.** $\frac{1}{2}$ cup
- **D.** 1 cup

17. Which of the following problems has the same mathematical structure as the problem given below?

> Selena had 7 pencils. She gave 2 pencils to her friend Amy. How many pencils does she have now?

   A) Selena brought 3 friends to the end-of-summer party. Amy brought 2 friends. How many friends did they bring together?
   B) Selena brought 10 carrot sticks for lunch. How many carrots sticks were left after she ate 6?
   C) Selena earned 2 stickers every school day this week, Monday through Friday. How many stickers did she earn?
   D) Selena has 7 markers. Amy has 3 more markers than Selena does. How many markers does Amy have?

18. Which of the following is listed in order from greatest to least?
   A) $\frac{1}{2}, \frac{1}{3}, \frac{1}{7}, -\frac{1}{5}, -\frac{1}{6}, -\frac{1}{4}$
   B) $\frac{1}{2}, \frac{1}{3}, \frac{1}{7}, -\frac{1}{6}, -\frac{1}{5}, -\frac{1}{4}$
   C) $\frac{1}{2}, \frac{1}{7}, \frac{1}{3}, -\frac{1}{4}, -\frac{1}{5}, -\frac{1}{6}$
   D) $\frac{1}{2}, \frac{1}{3}, \frac{1}{7}, -\frac{1}{6}, -\frac{1}{4}, -\frac{1}{5}$

19. Out of 1560 students at Ward Middle School, 15% want to take French. Which expression represents how many students want to take French?
   A) 1560 ÷ 15
   B) 1560 × 15
   C) 1560 × 0.15
   D) 1560 ÷ 0.15

20. Which of the following is closest to 15,886 × 210?
   A) 33,000
   B) 330,000
   C) 3,300,000
   D) 33,000,000

21. If the value of y is between 0.0047 and 0.0162, which of the following could be the value of y?
   A) 0.0035
   B) 0.0055
   C) 0.0185
   D) 0.0238

22. Which of the following is a solution to the inequality $2x + y \leq -10$?
   A) (0, 0)
   B) (10, 2)
   C) (10, 10)
   D) (−10, −10)

23. Justin has a summer lawn care business and earns $40 for each lawn he mows. He also pays $35 per week in business expenses. Which of the following expressions represents Justin's profit after x weeks if he mows m number of lawns?
   A) 40m − 35x
   B) 40m + 35x
   C) 35x(40 + m)
   D) 35(40m + x)

24. A baby weighed 7.5 pounds at birth and gained weight at a rate of 6 ounces per month for the first six months. Which equation describes the baby's weight in ounces, y, after t months?
   A) y = 6t + 7.5
   B) y = 6t + 120
   C) y = 7.5t + 120
   D) y = 7.5t + 7.5

25. Which expression is equivalent to 6x + 5 ≥ −15 + 8x?
   A) x ≤ −5
   B) x ≤ 5
   C) x ≤ 10
   D) x ≤ 20

26. Which of the following sequences follows the same rule as the sequence below?

   30, 27, 24, 21, ...

   A) 41, 39, 37, 35, ...
   B) 41, 44, 47, 50, ...
   C) 41, 37, 33, 29, ...
   D) 41, 38, 35, 32, ...

27. Students are asked if they prefer vanilla, chocolate, or strawberry ice cream. The results are tallied on the table below.

   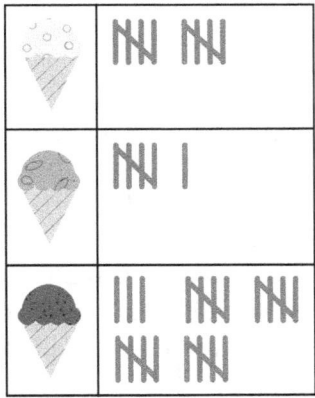

   Four students then display the information from the table in a bar graph. Which student completes the bar graph correctly?

   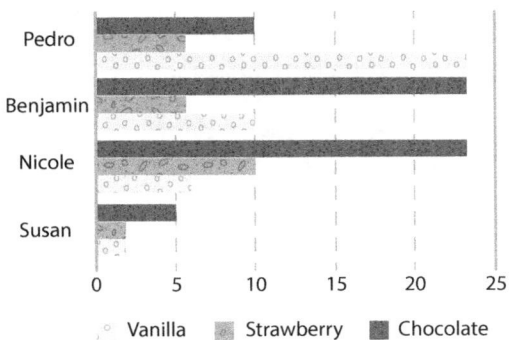

   A) Pedro
   B) Benjamin
   C) Nicole
   D) Susan

28.
   > If a + b is an even number, then both a and b must be even.

   Which of the following statements is a counterexample to the statement above?
   A) 6 + 9 = 15
   B) 8 + 3 = 11
   C) 10 + 14 = 24
   D) 17 + 15 = 32

29. Which of the following numbers is between $5\frac{1}{4}$ and $5\frac{1}{2}$?
   A) $5\frac{3}{4}$
   B) $5\frac{5}{8}$
   C) $5\frac{7}{20}$
   D) $5\frac{1}{10}$

30. A set of numbers contains all the prime factors of 42. What is the range of the set?
   A) 1
   B) 5
   C) 19
   D) 41

31. A circular swimming pool has a circumference of 50 feet. Which of the following is the diameter of the pool in feet?
   A) $\frac{25}{\pi}$
   B) $\frac{50}{\pi}$
   C) 25π
   D) 50π

32. If $4x = 3$, what is the value of $8x$?

A) 0.75
B) 6
C) 12
D) 24

33. The table below shows the number of hours employees worked during the week. Which of the following is the median number of hours the employees worked per week?

Employee	No. Hours Worked
Suzanne	42
Joe	38
Mark	26
Ellen	50
Jill	45
Rob	46
Nicole	17
Sean	41
Maria	46

A) 39
B) 41
C) 42
D) 46

34. Which graph shows $4x + 2 \geq 10$?

A)
B)
C)
D)

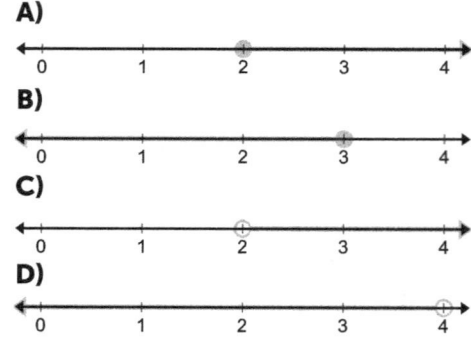

35. The pie graph below shows how a state's government plans to spend its annual budget of $3 billion. How much more money does the state plan to spend on infrastructure than education?

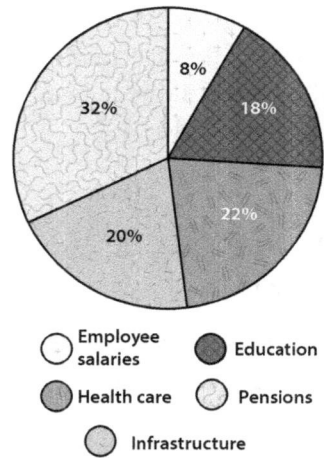

A) $60,000,000
B) $120,000,000
C) $300,000,000
D) $540,000,000

36. A company interviewed 21 applicants for a recent opening. Of these applicants, 7 wore blue and 6 wore white, while 5 applicants wore both blue and white. What is the number of applicants who wore neither blue nor white?

A) 6
B) 8
C) 12
D) 13

37. Which of the following numbers are equivalent to 2.61?

A) $\frac{261}{10}$
B) 2.061
C) $2\frac{61}{100}$
D) $2\frac{61}{1000}$

Practice Test One 81

Answer Key

1. **C)** The sum of three angles in any triangle is 180 degrees.

   Acute Triangle: three angles, all of which are less than 90 degrees.

   Right Triangle: one 90-degree angle and two angles less than 90 degrees.

   Regardless of the type, the sum of the angles will always equal 180 degrees, so the **two quantities are equal.**

2. **C)** Slope-intercept form, $y = mx + b$, with m = slope and b = y-intercept.

   Column A: the y-intercept is 0.

   Column B: the slope is 0.

   Therefore, **the two quantities are equal.**

3. **C)** Both MATH and FIRE have 4 letters with no letters repeating. There are 4 slots for the first letter, 3 slots for the second letter, 2 slots for the third letter, and 1 slot for the last letter.

   $4 \times 3 \times 2 \times 1 = 24$ unique ways to arrange the letters in both MATH and FIRE. **The two quantities are equal.**

4. **C)** Convert 30% to a decimal.

   30% = 0.3

   30% of 50 → 0.3 × 50 = 15

   Convert 50% to a decimal.

   50% = 0.5

   50% of 30 → 0.5 × 30 = 15

   The two quantities are equal.

5. **A)** With fractions, the larger the denominator, the smaller the value of the fraction.
   The value of x is between 0 and 1.

   For example, let $x = \frac{1}{2}$; $x^2 = \frac{1}{4}$ and $x^4 = \frac{1}{16}$.

   $\frac{1}{4} > \frac{1}{16}$

   The quantity in Column A is greater.

6. **B)** Both equations are written in slope-intercept form. The coefficient of x is the slope. Both have a slope of −1. For column B, the slope of a perpendicular line is the opposite reciprocal to the original line, so the slope of a line perpendicular to $y = -x - 2$ would be +1. **The quantity in Column B is greater.**

7. **D)** Three is greater than 4, but the value of the variables is unknown.

   If $a = 5$ and $b = 4$, then 3(5) = 15 and 4(4) = 16, making Column B greater.

   If $a = 7$ and $b = 2$, then 3(7) = 21 and 4(2) = 8, making Column A greater.

   The relationship cannot be determined from the information given.

8. **C)** There are 15 test scores, so the 8th score will be the median, which is 3.

   The score of 3 appears the most, 6 times, which makes it the mode as well.

   The two quantities are equal.

9. **C)** The triangles are congruent, so they have the same side lengths including the same base and height. The areas for both triangles are the same, so **the two quantities are equal.**

10. **B)** When adding 5 points to each test, the mean, median, and modes will all increase by 5 points.

    Mean = 83; Median = 88; Mode = 85

    If John's new test score is 87, then it is one point below the median score. Therefore, **the quantity in Column B is greater.**

11. **B)** In this function, we are told that $x \nabla y = 3x - y$. Plug in 2 and 3 to solve.

    $2 \nabla 3 = 3(2) - 3 = 6 - 3 = 3$.

    $3 \nabla 2 = 3(3) - 2 = 9 - 2 = 7$.

    $7 > 3$

    Therefore, **the quantity in Column B is greater.**

12. **D)** Multiply the exponents raised to a power.

    $\frac{(10^2)^3}{(10^{-2})^2} = \frac{10^6}{10^{-4}}$

    Subtract the exponent in the denominator from the exponent in the numerator.

    $10^{6-(-4)} = \mathbf{10^{10}}$

13. **D)** When adding 7 points to each test, the mean, median, and modes will all increase by 7 points.

    Mean = 85; Median = 81; Mode = 84

    The **range**, which is the difference between the lowest and highest score, will not change as a result of adding points.

14. **D)** The graph of $x = 3$ is a vertical line. It crosses the x-axis at 3 but **has an undefined slope.**

15. **D)** $400 \div 16 = 25$

    Simplify each expression and find the expression that equals 25.

    $2(200 - 8) = 2(192) = 384$

    $(400 \div 4) \div 12 = 100 \div 12 = 8.\overline{3}$

    $(216 \div 8) + (184 \div 8) = 27 + 23 = 50$

    $(216 \div 16) + (184 \div 16) = 13.5 + 11.5 = 25$

    $(216 \div 16) + (184 \div 16)$

16. **A)** $2\frac{1}{4}$ is divisible by $\frac{1}{4}$, so the $\frac{1}{4}$ cup can be used to measure the flour; $\frac{1}{4} \times 9 = 2\frac{1}{4}$.

17. **B)** The given problem is solved using subtraction: $7 - 2 = 5$ pencils. Problem B is also solved using subtraction: $10 - 6 = 4$ carrots.

    Selena brought 10 carrot sticks for lunch. How many carrots sticks were left after she ate 6?

18. **B)** Order the fractions by comparing the denominators.

    $\frac{1}{2} > \frac{1}{3} > \frac{1}{7} > -\frac{1}{6} > -\frac{1}{5} > -\frac{1}{4}$

19. **C)** Use the formula for finding percentages. Express the percentage as a decimal.

    part = whole × percentage

    part = **1560 × 0.15**

20. **C)** Round each number and multiply.

    $16{,}000 \times 200 = 3{,}200{,}000$
    ≈ **3,300,000**

21. **B)** Each of the decimal numbers are expressed in ten-thousandths. The number 55 is between 47 and 162, so **0.0055** is between 0.0047 and 0.0162.

22. **D)** Substitute each set of values and determine if the inequality is true.

    $(0, 0) \to 2(0) + 0 \leq -10$ FALSE

    $(10, 2) \to 2(10) + 2 \leq -10$ FALSE

    $(10, 10) \to 2(10) + 10 \leq -10$ FALSE

    $(-10, -10)$ $\to 2(-10) + (-10) \leq -10$ TRUE

23. **A)** Profit = income – expenses

    Income = $40 for each lawn, or $40m$.

    Expenses = $35 each week, or $35x$.

    Profit = **$40m - 35x$**

24. **B)** 1 pound = 16 ounces

    Birth weight $\to 7.5 \times 16 = 120$ ounces

    Gained 6 ounces per month, or $6t$.

    Current weight = monthly gain + birth weight

    $y = 6t + 120$

25. **C)** Isolate the variable on the left side of the inequality.

    $6x + 5 \geq -15 + 8x$

    $-2x + 5 \geq -15$

    $-2x \geq -20$

    Reverse the direction of the inequality when dividing by a negative number.

    $x \leq 10$

26. **D)** The given sequence is formed by subtracting 3. The new sequence would therefore start with 41 and decrease by 3 with each term: **41, 38, 35, 32, . . .**

27. **B)** The bar graph should show that 10 students prefer vanilla, 6 students prefer strawberry, and 23 students prefer chocolate ice cream. **Benjamin** completed the graph correctly.

28. **D)** A counterexample is an exception to a proposed general rule. The statement **17 + 15 = 32** is a counterexample because it shows that the sum of two odd numbers can be an even number.

29. **C)** Convert each fraction to a decimal.

    $5\frac{1}{4} = 5.25$

    $5\frac{1}{2} = 5.5$

    Convert each answer choice to a decimal to find a value between 5.25 and 5.5.

    $5\frac{7}{20}$ = 5.35, which is between 5.25 and 5.5.

30. **B)** Find all the factors of 42.

    $42 = 1 \times 42$

    $42 = 2 \times 21$

    $42 = 3 \times 14$

    $42 = 6 \times 7$

    The factors of 42 are 1, 2, 3, 6, 7, 14, 21, and 42.

    The prime factors are 2, 3, and 7. (1 is neither prime nor composite.)

    Subtract the smallest value from the largest to find the range.

    $7 - 2 = $ **5**

31. **B)** Circumference of a circle: $C = 2\pi r$.

    $d = 2r$, so $C = \pi d$.

    50 ft = πd

    $d = \frac{50}{\pi}$

32. **B)** Multiply each side by 2.

    $4x = 3$

    $2(4x) = 2(3)$

    $8x = $ **6**

33. C) Order the data from smallest to largest and find the middle value.

17, 26, 38, 41, **42**, 45, 46, 46, 50

34. A) Solve for x.

$4x + 2 \geq 10$

$4x + 2 - 2 \geq 10 - 2$

$4x \geq 8$

$\frac{4x}{4} \geq \frac{8}{4}$

$x \geq 2$

The graphed inequality has a **closed circle at 2,** and all values greater than 2 are shaded.

35. A) Find the amount the state will spend on infrastructure and education.

Infrastructure = 0.2(3,000,000,000) = 600,000,000

Education = 0.18(3,000,000,000) = 540,000,000

Find the difference.

600,000,000 – 540,000,000 = **$60,000,000**

36. D) Write an equation to find the number of people wearing neither white nor blue. Subtract the number of people wearing both colors so they are not counted twice.

total applicants = (applicants wearing blue) + (applicants wearing white) – (applicants wearing both blue and white) + (applicants wearing neither blue nor white)

21 = 7 + 6 – 5 + neither

neither = **13**

37. C) The decimal part ends in the hundredths place.

Place the decimal over 100 → $2\frac{61}{100}$.

Practice Test One 85

Reading Comprehension

> The greatest changes in sensory, motor, and perceptual development happen in the first two years of life. When babies are first born, most of their senses operate like those of adults. For example, babies are able to hear before they are born; studies show that babies turn toward the sound of their mothers' voices just minutes after being born, indicating they recognize the mother's voice from their time in the womb.
>
> The exception to this rule is vision. A baby's vision changes significantly in the first year of life; initially a baby has a vision range of only 8 – 12 inches and no depth perception. As a result, infants rely primarily on hearing; vision does not become the dominant sense until around the age of twelve months. Babies also prefer faces to other objects. This preference, along with their limited vision range, means that their sight is initially focused on their caregiver.

1. The primary purpose of the passage is to
   A) compare vision in adults to vision in newborns.
   B) persuade readers to get their infants' eyes checked.
   C) confirm a recent scientific finding about senses.
   D) explain how an infant's senses operate and change.

2. According to the passage, when does vision become the dominant sense?
   A) at birth
   B) around twelve months of age
   C) when hearing declines
   D) at adulthood

3. Newborns mostly rely on
   A) vision.
   B) touch.
   C) taste.
   D) hearing.

4. What is the main idea of this passage?
   A) The senses of babies operate like the senses of adults.
   B) Babies have a limited vision range and rely on hearing for their first months of life.
   C) Babies prefer faces to other objects due to their small range of vision in the early months.
   D) Studies show that babies turn toward the sound of their mothers' voices after being born.

5. What evidence does the author provide to support his claim that babies are able to hear before they are born?
   A) The greatest changes in sensory development happen in the first two years of life.
   B) Vision does not become the dominant sense until around the age of twelve months.
   C) Babies turn toward the sound of their mothers' voices just minutes after being born.
   D) When babies are born, most of their senses operate like those of adults.

> Geography is the study of space. More specifically, it studies the physical space of Earth and how the planet interacts with, shapes, and is shaped by people and animals. Geographers look at the world from a spatial perspective. In other words, geographers are always asking the question, "Where?" For geographers, where any interaction, event, or development happens is the key to understanding it.
>
> There are many subdisciplines of geography. These can be organized into four main categories. Regional Studies looks at the characteristics of a particular place. Topical Studies looks at a single physical or human feature that impacts the whole world. Physical Studies focuses on the physical features of Earth. Human Studies examines the relationship between human activity and the environment.

6. What is the subdiscipline of geography that looks at the impact of a single physical or human feature on the world?
   A) Regional Studies
   B) Topical Studies
   C) Physical Studies
   D) Human Studies

7. What is the topic of this passage?
   A) human activity
   B) spatial perspective
   C) geography
   D) Earth

8. Which of the following would Physical Studies most likely examine?
   A) the causes of migration during a drought
   B) the impact of pollution on human beings
   C) the height of various mountain ranges around the world
   D) the characteristics of a particular region in a country

9. Geographers ask the question "Where?" because
   A) geographers think about the world through a spatial perspective.
   B) geography includes the subdiscipline of human studies.
   C) it is asked in a variety of fields of study, not just geographic.
   D) humans interact with various aspects of their world every day.

It could be said that the great battle between the North and South we call the Civil War was a battle for individual identity. The states of the South had their own culture, one based on farming, independence, and the right of both man and state to determine their own paths. Similarly, the North had forged its own identity as a center of centralized commerce and manufacturing. This clash of lifestyles was bound to create tension, and this tension was bound to lead to war. But people who try to sell you this narrative are wrong. The Civil War was not a battle of cultural identities—it was a battle about slavery. All other explanations for the war are either a direct consequence of the South's desire for wealth at the expense of her fellow man or a fanciful invention to cover up this sad portion of our nation's history. And it cannot be denied that this time in our past was very sad indeed.

10. The author believes people say the war was fought because of a clash in cultural identities because they
    A) want to avoid acknowledging the shameful parts of the United States' history.
    B) do not believe the Civil War was actually fought between the North and the South.
    C) are trying to make a better future for the United States despite its past.
    D) hope to promote the cause of the North instead of the South.

11. What is the topic of the passage?
    A) individual identity
    B) slavery
    C) the cause of the Civil War
    D) desire for wealth

12. According to the passage, which of the following is the reason the Civil War was fought?
    A) cultural differences
    B) the South's desire for wealth
    C) slavery
    D) individual identity

13. What is the tone of this passage?
    A) hopeful
    B) humorous
    C) cautious
    D) assertive

14. Based on the information from the passage, a person from the North during the time of the Civil War would most likely
    A) work in manufacturing.
    B) oppose the Civil War.
    C) be a farmer.
    D) have enslaved people.

CONTINUE

Skin coloration and markings have an important role to play in the world of snakes. Those intricate diamonds, stripes, and swirls help the animals hide from predators, but perhaps most importantly (for us humans, anyway), markings can also indicate whether the snake is venomous. While it might seem <u>counterintuitive</u> for a venomous snake to stand out in bright red or blue, that fancy costume tells any nearby predator that approaching it would be a bad idea.

If you see a flashy-looking snake in the woods, though, those markings don't necessarily mean it's venomous: some snakes have found a way to ward off predators without the actual venom. The scarlet kingsnake, for example, has very similar markings to the venomous coral snake with whom it frequently shares a habitat. However, the kingsnake is actually nonvenomous; it's merely pretending to be dangerous to eat. A predatory hawk or eagle, usually hunting from high in the sky, can't tell the difference between the two species, so the kingsnake gets passed over and lives another day.

15. What is this passage primarily about?
- A) snake habitats
- B) predators of snakes
- C) snake coloration and markings
- D) venomous and nonvenomous snakes

16. According to the passage, which of the following is TRUE about the scarlet kingsnake?
- A) It is venomous to predators.
- B) It often lives in the same areas as the coral snake.
- C) It is dangerous to a hawk or eagle.
- D) It is difficult to eat.

17. According to the passage, what is true about venomous snakes?
- A) They have markings that camouflage them from predators.
- B) They pretend to be nonvenomous when predators are around.
- C) They can be a threat to nonvenomous snakes.
- D) They can be identified by markings on their skin.

18. A predatory eagle may pass over a kingsnake because the kingsnake
- A) is venomous.
- B) can be easily mistaken for a venomous snake.
- C) blends in with its environment.
- D) is not as nutritious to the eagle as other snakes.

19. Based on the passage, what does *counterintuitive* most likely mean?
- A) contrary to common belief
- B) similar in meaning
- C) difficult to understand
- D) a wise decision

Taking a person's temperature is one of the most basic and common health care tasks. Everyone from nurses to emergency medical technicians to concerned parents should be able to grab a thermometer and take a patient's or loved one's temperature. But what's the best way to get an accurate reading? The answer depends on the situation.

The most common way people measure body temperature is orally. A simple digital or disposable thermometer is placed under the tongue for a few minutes, and the task is done. There are many situations, however, when measuring temperature orally isn't an option. For example, when a person can't breathe through her nose, she won't be able to keep her mouth closed long enough to get an accurate reading. In these situations, it's often preferable to place the thermometer in the rectum or armpit. Using the rectum also has the added benefit of providing a much more accurate reading than other locations can provide.

It's also often the case that certain people, like agitated patients or fussy babies, won't be able to sit still long enough for an accurate reading. In these situations, it's best to use a thermometer that works much more quickly, such as one that measures temperature in the ear or at the temporal artery. No matter which method is chosen, however, it's important to check the average temperature for each region, as it can vary by several degrees.

20. What is the main idea of this passage?
  A) The best way to take a temperature is by placing the thermometer under the tongue.
  B) Taking a temperature is a very simple task.
  C) Some ways to take a temperature are more beneficial in certain situations.
  D) It is especially difficult to get an accurate temperature reading on children.

21. Why is measuring one's temperature in the ear or at the temporal artery beneficial?
  A) The situation determines the best way to get an accurate temperature reading.
  B) Some patients are not able to sit still long enough for an oral temperature reading.
  C) Everyone should be able to take a patient's or loved one's temperature.
  D) These regions provide a much more accurate reading than other locations.

22. What is the structure of this text?
  A) cause and effect
  B) order and sequence
  C) problem and solution
  D) compare and contrast

23. Taking a temperature at the temporal artery
  A) is most accurate when done by a medical doctor.
  B) is the best way to get an accurate reading.
  C) will result in a different degree reading from under the tongue.
  D) will result in the same degree reading as from the ear.

24. According to the passage, what is the most common way to take a person's temperature?
  A) under the tongue
  B) in the armpit
  C) in the ear
  D) at the temporal artery

25. According to the text, taking a temperature
  A) is a simple task that most adults should be able to do.
  B) can be dangerous if the result is not read correctly.
  C) should be left up to medical professionals like nurses.
  D) will give consistent results regardless of where it is taken.

We've been told for years that the recipe for weight loss is fewer calories in than out. In other words, eat less and exercise more, and your body will take care of the rest. As many who've tried to diet can attest, this <u>edict</u> doesn't always produce results. If you're one of those folks, you might have felt that you just weren't doing it right—that the failure was all your fault.

However, several new studies released this year have suggested that it might not be your fault at all. For example, a study of people who'd lost a high percentage of their body weight (more than 17 percent) in a short period of time found that they could not physically maintain their new weight. Scientists measured their resting metabolic rate and found that they'd need to consume only a few hundred calories a day to meet their metabolic needs. Basically, their bodies were in starvation mode and seemed to desperately hang on to each and every calorie. Eating even a single healthy, well-balanced meal a day would cause these subjects to start packing the pounds back on.

Other studies have shown that factors like intestinal bacteria, distribution of body fat, and hormone levels can affect the manner in which our bodies process calories.
There's also the fact that it's actually quite difficult to measure the number of calories consumed during a particular meal and the number used while exercising.

---

26. Which of the following is this passage chiefly concerned with?
  A) calories
  B) exercise
  C) weight loss
  D) metabolic needs

27. According to the text, people who lose a high percentage of their body weight in a short period of time may
  A) gain more than 17 percent of their body weight back after returning to a normal diet.
  B) continue to lose weight if they maintain their normal diet.
  C) be susceptible to high levels of intestinal bacteria.
  D) start gaining the weight back even with healthy eating habits.

28. According to the text, which of the following is true about hormone levels?

- **A)** They can impact a person's ability to lose weight.
- **B)** They will change based on a person's diet.
- **C)** They make a person think he is losing weight even if he is not.
- **D)** They were the subject of a new study released this year.

29. Based on the text, what does *edict* most likely mean?

- **A)** hormone
- **B)** rule
- **C)** relationship
- **D)** diet

30. Why did the author most likely write this text?

- **A)** to inform the reader about potential causes of inconsistencies in weight loss
- **B)** to persuade others to practice traditional dieting techniques
- **C)** to warn against losing a high percentage of body weight quickly
- **D)** to compare and contrast the effects of dieting to the effects of exercise

---

In recent decades, jazz has been associated with New Orleans and festivals like Mardi Gras, but in the 1920s, jazz was a booming trend whose influence reached into many aspects of American culture. In fact, the years between World War I and the Great Depression were known as the Jazz Age, a term coined by F. Scott Fitzgerald in his famous novel *The Great Gatsby*. Sometimes also called the Roaring Twenties, this time period saw major urban centers experiencing new economic, cultural, and artistic vitality. In the United States, musicians flocked to cities like New York and Chicago, which would become famous hubs for jazz musicians. Ella Fitzgerald, for example, moved from Virginia to New York City to begin her much-lauded singing career, and jazz pioneer Louis Armstrong got his big break in Chicago.

Jazz music was played by and for a more expressive and freed populace than the United States had previously seen. Women gained the right to vote and were openly seen drinking and dancing to jazz music. This period marked the emergence of the flapper, a woman determined to make a statement about her new role in society. Jazz music also provided the soundtrack for the explosion of African American art and culture now known as the Harlem Renaissance. In addition to Fitzgerald and Armstrong, numerous musicians, including Duke Ellington, Fats Waller, and Bessie Smith, promoted their distinctive and complex music as an integral part of the emerging African American culture.

---

31. According to the passage, what did cities experience during the Roaring Twenties?

- **A)** the Great Depression
- **B)** economic, cultural, and artistic vitality
- **C)** festivals like Mardi Gras
- **D)** an increase in women living there

32. According to the passage, where is jazz is most likely to be heard today?
- A) Chicago
- B) New York City
- C) New Orleans
- D) Los Angeles

33. The Jazz Age is also known as the
- A) Great Gatsby.
- B) Mardi Gras.
- C) Roaring Twenties.
- D) Harlem Renaissance.

34. According to the passage, which of the following was true about cities during the Jazz Age?
- A) They became famous hubs for jazz musicians.
- B) They were abandoned because of the Great Depression.
- C) They saw an increase in African Americans living there.
- D) They struggled economically compared to rural areas.

35. What evidence does the author provide to support the claim that jazz music was played by and for a more expressive and freed populace?
- A) Jazz was a booming trend whose influence reached into many aspects of American culture.
- B) This time period saw urban centers experiencing new economic, cultural, and artistic vitality.
- C) The years between World War I and the Great Depression were known as the *Jazz Age*.
- D) Women gained the right to vote and were openly seen drinking and dancing to jazz music.

36. What is the main idea of this passage?
- A) Jazz influenced many aspects of American culture during the 1920s.
- B) The Harlem Renaissance was the explosion of African American art and culture.
- C) Today jazz is mostly associated with New Orleans and festivals like Mardi Gras.
- D) F. Scott Fitzgerald coined the term *Jazz Age* to describe the time after World War I.

Answer Key

1. **D)** The passage explains how an infant's senses operate while specifically detailing the changes experienced with vision.

2. **B)** The passage states that vision does not become the dominant sense until around the age of twelve months.

3. **D)** The passage explains that infants rely primarily on hearing because vision does not become a dominant sense until around the age of twelve months.

4. **B)** The passage specifically explains the changes an infant experiences in vision and that because of this late development, hearing is a dominant sense at first.

5. **C)** The author explains that studies show that babies turn toward the sound of their mothers' voices just minutes after being born, indicating that an infant recognizes the mother's voice from their time in the womb. This evidence supports the claim that babies are able to hear before they are born.

6. **B)** The author states that Topical Studies looks at a single physical or human feature that impacts the whole world.

7. **C)** This passage focuses on geography and its purpose.

8. **C)** Physical studies focus on the physical features (mountain ranges) of Earth.

9. **A)** Geography is the study of space, which means geographers think about space, place, and location. They consider where something happens.

10. **A)** The author says that any explanation for the cause of the Civil War that does not involve slavery is just a fanciful invention to cover up this sad portion of our nation's history. This implies that people do not want to admit something so shameful happened.

11. **C)** The passage explores proposed causes of the Civil War, which are represented in the other answer choices.

12. **C)** The author says, "The Civil War was not a battle of cultural identities—it was a battle about slavery."

13. **D)** The author writes this passage to correct misinformation on the topic of the causes of the Civil War. He writes with an assertive, or self-confident, tone, insisting that his interpretation of this historical event is accurate while the others are wrong. For example, he says, "People who try to sell you this narrative are wrong," showing his confidence in his position and his disdain for others' opinions on this topic.

14. **A)** The text explains that the North had "forged its own identity as the center of centralized commerce and manufacturing."

15. **C)** This passage explains how the snake's coloration and markings help it hide from predators while also warning humans and predators that it may be venomous.

16. **B)** The author explains that the scarlet kingsnake and coral snake frequently share a habitat.

17. **D)** The author explains that the markings on a snake can indicate whether a snake is venomous.

18. **B)** The author explains that the markings of a kingsnake are very similar to those of a venomous coral snake. The coral snake is dangerous to a predatory eagle, so the eagle avoids eating the kingsnake for fear it is a coral snake.

19. **A)** The text says, "It might seem counterintuitive for a venomous snake to stand out in bright red or blue," meaning that it seems like a venomous snake would want to stay hidden from predators. However, the text continues by explaining that venomous snakes actually can have vivid skin colors and prints to ward off predators, so *counterintuitive* means "contrary to common belief."

20. **C)** The article explains the many ways a temperature can be taken. It also tells which methods are most useful and reliable in various situations.

21. **B)** The author explains that while taking a temperature orally is most common, many patients are not able to sit still for the length of time it takes to get an accurate reading. Using one's ear or temporal artery is quicker and therefore beneficial in these situations.

22. **D)** In this text, the various methods of measuring temperatures are being compared and contrasted to answer the question, "What is the best way to get an accurate reading?"

23. **C)** The author explains that it is important to check the average temperature for each region, as it can vary by several degrees.

24. **A)** The text states that the most common way people take someone's temperature is orally, and the author goes on to clarify that the correct location of the oral thermometer is under the tongue.

25. **A)** The first paragraph of the text explains that taking a temperature is a basic medical procedure that can be done by nearly anyone, including a parent.

26. **C)** The passage explains weight loss and how each of the other answer choices impact one's ability to lose weight.

27. **D)** The text says that in some cases people who lose a high percentage of their body weight in a short period of time cannot physically maintain their new weight, and as a result, their body will desperately hang on to calories resulting in weight gain even with a healthy diet.

28. **A)** The text says that hormone levels can affect the way our bodies process calories, which impacts a person's ability to lose weight.

29. **B)** The text uses the word *edict* to refer to the commonly understood rule of dieting that says an individual must burn more calories than he or she takes in.

30. **A)** The text explains that following a traditional model for calorie intake may not always produce results because of several factors that may interfere with the weight loss process.

31. **B)** The passage says that urban centers experienced new economic, cultural, and artistic vitality.

32. **C)** The passage explains that recently jazz has been associated with New Orleans.

33. **C)** The author explains that the Jazz Age was sometimes called the Roaring Twenties.

34. **A)** The text says musicians flocked to cities like New York and Chicago, which became famous hubs for jazz musicians.

35. **D)** Because women had recently gained the right to vote, the author refers to them as part of the more expressive and freed populace who listened to jazz music. Although the other options are true, they are not details that support this specific claim.

36. **A)** While each of the answer choices are facts from the passage, the main idea of the passage as a whole is that jazz had a significant impact on various parts of American culture during the 1920s.

Mathematical Achievement

1. What number is equal to $(5^2 + 1)^2 + 3^3$?
   A) 703
   B) 694
   C) 53
   D) 30

2. If $x = 5$, what is the value of the algebraic expression $2x - x$?
   A) 5
   B) 10
   C) 15
   D) 20

3. Simplify: $\dfrac{7.2 \times 10^6}{1.6 \times 10^{-3}}$
   A) 4.5×10^{-9}
   B) 4.5×10^{-3}
   C) 4.5×10^3
   D) 4.5×10^9

4. A high school cross-country team sent 25 percent of its runners to a regional competition. Of these, 10 percent won medals. If two runners earned medals, how many members does the cross-country team have?
   A) 8
   B) 80
   C) 125
   D) 1250

5. A teacher has 50 notebooks to hand out to students. If she has 16 students in her class, and each student receives two notebooks, how many notebooks will she have left over?
   A) 2
   B) 16
   C) 18
   D) 32

6. 40% of what number is equal to 17?
   A) 2.35
   B) 6.8
   C) 42.5
   D) 680

7. An ice chest contains 24 sodas, some regular and some diet. The ratio of diet soda to regular soda is 1:3. How many regular sodas are there in the ice chest?
   A) 1
   B) 4
   C) 18
   D) 24

8. In the sequence below, each term is the difference between the previous two numbers and multiplying the result by −3. What is the 6th term of the sequence?
   {3, 0, −9, −36, ...}
   A) −135
   B) −81
   C) 81
   D) 135

9. If a car uses 8 gallons of gas to travel 650 miles, how many miles can it travel using 12 gallons of gas?
   A) 870 miles
   B) 895 miles
   C) 915 miles
   D) 975 miles

10. If $j = 4$, what is the value of $2(j - 4)^4 - j + \frac{1}{2}j$?
    A) −2
    B) 0
    C) 2
    D) 4

11. Which of the following is equivalent to $54z^4 + 18z^3 + 3z + 3$?

    A) $18z^4 + 6z^3 + z + 1$
    B) $3z(18z^3 + 6z^2 + 1)$
    C) $72z^7 + 3z$
    D) $3(18z^4 + 6z^3 + z + 1)$

12. The formula for distance is $d = r \times t$, where r is the rate and t is the time. How long will it take a plane to fly 4000 miles from Chicago to London if the plane flies at a constant rate of 500 mph?

    A) 3.5 hours
    B) 8 hours
    C) 20 hours
    D) 45 hours

13. How much water is needed to fill 24 bottles that each hold 0.75 liters?

    A) 6 L
    B) 18 L
    C) 24 L
    D) 32 L

14. Yanni bought a used car. He made a down payment of $3000 and then made monthly payments of $216 for three years. How much did Yanni pay for the car?

    A) $10,776
    B) $7806
    C) $7776
    D) $3678

15. The perimeter of a rectangle is 42 mm. If the length of the rectangle is 13 mm, what is its width?

    A) 8 mm
    B) 13 mm
    C) 20 mm
    D) 29 mm

16. If the volume of a cube is 343 cubic meters, what is the cube's surface area?

    A) 49 m²
    B) 84 m²
    C) 196 m²
    D) 294 m²

17. A table is 150 centimeters long. How many millimeters long is the table?

    A) 1.5 mm
    B) 15 mm
    C) 150 mm
    D) 1500 mm

18. If $\mathbf{B} = \begin{bmatrix} 6 & 4 & 8 \\ -2 & 5 & -3 \end{bmatrix}$ and $\mathbf{C} = \begin{bmatrix} -2 & 5 & 7 \\ 1 & -4 & 4 \end{bmatrix}$, find $\mathbf{B} + \mathbf{C}$.

    A) $\begin{bmatrix} 4 & 9 & 15 \\ -1 & -1 & -1 \end{bmatrix}$
    B) $\begin{bmatrix} 4 & 9 & 15 \\ -1 & 1 & 1 \end{bmatrix}$
    C) $\begin{bmatrix} 4 & 9 & 15 \\ 1 & 1 & 1 \end{bmatrix}$
    D) $\begin{bmatrix} -4 & -9 & -15 \\ 1 & -1 & -1 \end{bmatrix}$

19. In a class of 20 students, how many conversations must take place so that every student talks to every other student in the class?

    A) 190
    B) 380
    C) 760
    D) 6840

20. A school held a raffle to raise money. If a person who bought 3 tickets had a 0.0004 chance of

winning, what is the total number of tickets sold for the raffle?

A) 2400 tickets
B) 3500 tickets
C) 5000 tickets
D) 7500 tickets

21. The figure below shows a rectangle with 4 square cutouts made to each corner. What is the area of the resulting shape?

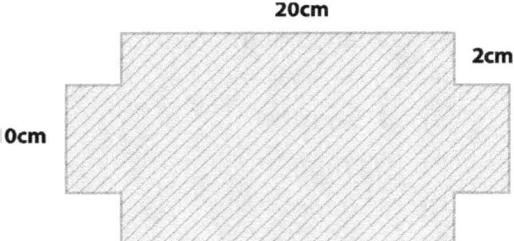

A) 142 cm²
B) 200 cm²
C) 296 cm²
D) 320 cm²

22. Melissa is ordering fencing to enclose a square garden with 5625 square feet. Which of the following is the number of feet of fencing she needs?

A) 75
B) 150
C) 300
D) 1405

23. Juan is packing a shipment of three books weighing 0.8 pounds, 0.49 pounds, and 0.89 pounds. The maximum weight for the shipping box is 2.5 pounds. How much more weight will the box hold?

A) 0.32 lb
B) 0.48 lb
C) 1.21 lb
D) 2.18 lb

24. The circle below shows a walking path through a park. If the distance from A to B is 4 km, how far will someone travel when they walk along arc AB?

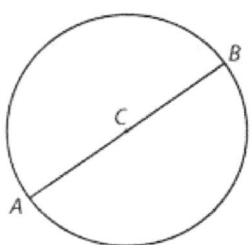

A) 4 km
B) 2π km
C) 8 km
D) 4π km

25. How many combinations can be made from a wardrobe that consists of 70 shirts, 2 ties, and 5 sets of cufflinks?

A) 77
B) 350
C) 700
D) 3500

26. A python coils 6 times around a round plastic bucket whose radius is 5 inches. How long is the python? (Round to the nearest whole number.)

A) 471 inches
B) 188 inches
C) 94 inches
D) 60 inches

Practice Test One 101

27. An executive board plans to host meetings for 5 hours and 45 minutes. They want to include an hour lunchbreak plus two 20-minute breaks. If they must leave by 3:30 p.m., what time should the conference begin?

A) 9:45 a.m.
B) 9:05 a.m.
C) 8:05 a.m.
D) 4:35 a.m.

28. The final grade in a college course is determined by the score on the midterm and final exam. The final exam score is weighted double the midterm. If a student scores 92 on the midterm, and the lowest A is a 90 with no rounding, what is the lowest score they can earn on the final exam and still receive an A?

A) 86
B) 88
C) 89
D) 90

29. Freedom Junior High School has a student council with 27 members and must choose officers to serve as president, vice president, and secretary. Six students intend to run for office. The president will be elected first, then the vice president, and then the secretary. How many different ways can these offices be filled?

A) 15
B) 78
C) 120
D) 17,550

30. A 6-screen movie theater decides to set 3 of its screens to show the newest movie. The theater operates between 11 a.m. and 9 p.m., and the film lasts 1 hour and 30 minutes. If there must be at least 30 minutes between showings to clean the theater, how many times can the theater show the film each day?

A) 16
B) 15
C) 12
D) 5

31. In a game of musical chairs, there are 9 people playing and 7 available seats. Those who do not get a seat by the time the music ends are eliminated. What is the probability a person is not eliminated?

A) 11%
B) 22%
C) 78%
D) 89%

32. Pauline is running for class historian. All 175 students voted in the election, and she received 40% of the vote. How many students voted for Pauline?

A) 40
B) 70
C) 135
D) 438

33. Tamara is hosting a birthday party at the movie theater. Her mother gives her $50 to spend on movie tickets for her friends. The theater charges $4 per person and a $6 service charge for the order. How many friends can she invite to the party?

  A) 5
  B) 11
  C) 12
  D) 40

34. A movie runs for 92 minutes. For it to air on television, it must be edited down to 88 minutes to make room for commercials. What percent of the movie must be edited?

  A) Between 2 and 3%
  B) Between 3 and 4%
  C) Between 4 and 5%
  D) Between 5 and 6%

35. A sandwich shop offers 4 different types of meat, 3 types of cheese, 2 types of bread, and 4 condiments. If each sandwich must have 1 meat, 1 cheese, 1 type of bread, and 1 condiment, how many different sandwiches can be made?

  A) 13
  B) 32
  C) 96
  D) 300

36. A car traveled at 65 miles per hour for $1\frac{1}{2}$ hours and then traveled at 50 miles per hour for $2\frac{1}{2}$ hours. How many miles did the car travel?

  A) 200 miles
  B) 222.5 miles
  C) 237.5 miles
  D) 260 miles

37. Justine bought 6 yards of fabric to make some curtains, but she only used $4\frac{5}{8}$ yards. How many yards of fabric does she have left?

  A) $\frac{3}{8}$
  B) $\frac{5}{8}$
  C) $1\frac{3}{8}$
  D) $2\frac{5}{8}$

38. Alice ran $3\frac{1}{2}$ miles on Monday, and she increased her distance by $\frac{1}{4}$ mile each day. What was her total distance from Monday to Friday?

  A) $17\frac{1}{2}$ mi
  B) $18\frac{1}{2}$ mi
  C) 19 mi
  D) 20 mi

39. A doctor advises her patient to decrease his sugar consumption by 25%. If he currently consumes 40 grams of sugar per day on average, how many daily grams of sugar should his new target be?

  A) 30 g
  B) 24 g
  C) 16 g
  D) 10 g

40. Andre welded together 3 pieces of metal pipe measuring 26.5 inches, 18.9 inches, and 35.1 inches. How long was the welded pipe?

  A) 10.3 in
  B) 27.5 in
  C) 42.7 in
  D) 80.5 in

41. Solve: $-4x + 2 = -34$
   A) -9
   B) -8
   C) 8
   D) 9

42. Bob's hospital bill is $1896. If Bob pays $158 per month, which expression represents his balance after x months?
   A) $1896 - 158x$
   B) $158x + 1896$
   C) $1738x$
   D) $158(1896 - x)$

43. Harvey types at an average speed of 45 words per minute. Approximately how long will it take for him to type a newsletter that is 4500 words in length?
   A) 89 minutes
   B) 100 minutes
   C) 180 minutes
   D) 3955 minutes

44. Mr. Osborne grades a math test and finds that the mean score is 75%, the median score is 72%, the mode score is 83%, and the range is 25. If he wants the average to be equivalent to a B−, or 81%, then how many points should he add to each of the tests?
   A) 3
   B) 6
   C) 8
   D) 9

45. A map has a scale of 1 inch to 25 miles. What is the distance on the map between two towns that are 125 miles apart?
   A) 0.2 inches
   B) 1 inch
   C) 5 inches
   D) 25 inches

46. The average traffic light cycle at an intersection is $2\frac{1}{2}$ minutes, and 12 cars go through the intersection during each green light. If Martin must wait $7\frac{1}{2}$ minutes to cross the intersection, which of the following could be the number of cars ahead of him?
   A) 4
   B) 10
   C) 30
   D) 120

47. A computer store sells both laptops and desktops. On Sunday, the store sold three times as many laptops as desktops. If the store sold a total of 56 computers, how many more laptops did it sell than desktops?
   A) 14
   B) 28
   C) 37
   D) 42

Answer Key

1. **A)** Use order of operations to simplify the expression.
   $(5^2 + 1)^2 + 3^3 \rightarrow (25 + 1)^2 + 3^3 \rightarrow 676 + 27 \rightarrow$ **703**

2. **A)** Substitute 5 for x.
   $2(5) - 5 \rightarrow 10 - 5 =$ **5**

3. **D)**
   $\frac{7.2 \times 10^6}{1.6 \times 10^{-3}}$
   Divide the decimals.
   $7.2 \div 1.6 = 4.5$
   Subtract the exponents.
   $6 - (-3) = 9$
   4.5×10^9

4. **B)** Work backwards and write a proportion to find the number of runners in the competition (c).
   $\frac{2}{c} = \frac{10}{100}$
   $c = 20$
   Substitute to find the number of runners on the team (r).
   $\frac{20}{r} = \frac{25}{100}$
   $r =$ **80**

5. **C)** Each student receives 2 notebooks.
   $16 \times 2 = 32$ notebooks
   Subtract to determine the notebooks that are left.
   $50 - 32 =$ **18** notebooks left

6. **C)** Use the equation for percentages.
   whole $= \frac{part}{percent} = \frac{17}{0.4} =$ **42.5**

7. **C)**
   Set up a proportion.
   $\frac{Regular}{Total} \rightarrow \frac{3}{4} = \frac{x}{24}$
   Cross multiply.
   $4x = 72$
   $x =$ **18**

8. **A)** Find the 5th term.
   The difference between the previous two numbers.
   $-9 - (-36) = 27$
   Multiply the result by -3.
   $27(-3) = -81$
   Find the 6th term.
   The difference between the previous two numbers.
   $-36 - (-81) = 45$
   Multiply the result by -3.
   $45(-3) =$ **-135**

9. **D)** Set up a proportion and solve.
   $\frac{8}{650} = \frac{12}{x}$
   Cross multiply.
   $12(650) = 8x$
   $x =$ **975 miles**

10. **A)** Substitute 4 for j and simplify.
    $2(j - 4)^4 - j + \frac{1}{2}j$
    $2(4 - 4)^4 - 4 + \frac{1}{2}(4)$
    $2(0) - 4 + 2 =$ **-2**

11. **D)** Factor the expression using the greatest common factor of 3.
    $54z^4 + 18z^3 + 3z + 3 =$ **$3(18z^4 + 6z^3 + z + 1)$**

12. **B)** Substitute the given values into the equation and solve for t.
    $d = r \times t$
    $4000 = 500 \times t$
    $t =$ **8 hours**

Practice Test One

13. **B)** Multiply the number of bottles by the amount each holds.

    $24 \times 0.75 = \mathbf{18}$

14. **A)** 1 year = 12 months

    3 years = 3 × 12 = 36 monthly payments.

    Down payment + months paid × monthly payment = total paid

    $\$3000 + 36(\$216) \rightarrow \$3000 + \$7776 = \mathbf{\$10{,}776}$

15. **A)** Use the equation for the perimeter of a rectangle.

    $P = 2l + 2w$

    $42 = 2(13) + 2w$

    $w = \mathbf{8}$

16. **D)** Use the volume to find the length of the cube's side.

    $V = s^3$

    $343 = s^3$

    $s = 7$ m

    Find the area of each side.

    $7(7) = 49$ m²

    Multiply by the total number of sides, 6, to find the total surface area.

    $49(6) = \mathbf{294}$ **m²**

17. **D)** Use dimensional analysis to convert centimeters to millimeters.

    $150 \text{ cm} \times \frac{10 \text{ mm}}{1 \text{ cm}} = \mathbf{1500 \text{ mm}}$

18. **B)** Add the corresponding parts of each matrix.

    $\begin{bmatrix} 6 & 4 & 8 \\ -2 & 5 & -3 \end{bmatrix} + \begin{bmatrix} -2 & 5 & 7 \\ 1 & -4 & 4 \end{bmatrix}$

    $= \begin{bmatrix} 6+(-2) & 4+5 & 8+7 \\ -2+1 & 5+(-4) & -3+4 \end{bmatrix}$

    $= \begin{bmatrix} \mathbf{4} & \mathbf{9} & \mathbf{15} \\ \mathbf{-1} & \mathbf{1} & \mathbf{1} \end{bmatrix}$

19. **A)** Use the combination formula to find the number of ways to choose 2 people out of a group of 20.

    $C(20, 2) \rightarrow \frac{20!}{2!18!} \rightarrow \frac{(20)(19)}{2} = \mathbf{190}$

20. **D)** Rearrange the formula for probability to solve for the number of possible outcomes.

    $P = \frac{\text{number of favorable outcomes}}{\text{number of possible outcomes}}$

    number of possible outcomes = $\frac{\text{number of favorable outcomes}}{P}$

    number of possible outcomes = $\frac{3}{0.0004} = \mathbf{7500}$

21. **D)** Find the area of the complete rectangle.

    rectangle: $A = lw = (20 + 2 + 2) \times (10 + 2 + 2) = 336$ cm²

    corners: $A = 4(lw) = 4(2 \times 2) = 16$ cm²

    Subtract the area of the missing corners.

    $336 - 16 = \mathbf{320}$ **cm²**

22. **C)** Use the area formula to find the length of one side of the square.

    $A = s^2$

    $5{,}625 = s^2$

    $\sqrt{5{,}625} = s$

    $s = 75$ ft

    Multiply the side length by 4 to find the perimeter.

    $P = 4s$

    $P = 4(75 \text{ ft}) = \mathbf{300 \text{ ft}}$

23. A) Find the total weight of the three books.

0.8 + 0.49 + 0.89 = 2.18 lb

Subtract the weight of the books from the maximum weight for the shipping box.

2.5 − 2.18 = **0.32 lb**

24. B) Find the circle's radius.

4 km ÷ 2 = 2 km

Use the radius to find the circumference of the circle.

$C = 2\pi r = 2\pi(2) = 4\pi$

Arc AB is a semicircle, which means its length is half the circumference of the circle.

$\frac{4\pi}{2} =$ **2π km**

25. C) Multiply the number of outcomes for each individual event.

(70)(2)(5) = **700** outfits

26. B) Find the circumference of the bucket.

If $r = 5$ inches, then $C = 2\pi(5) = 10\pi$ or 31.4 inches.

The python coils around the bucket six times. Multiply the circumference by 6.

31.4 × 6 = 188.4 ≈ **188 inches**

27. C) Rewrite the ending time of 3:30 p.m. as 15:30. The meetings last 5 hours and 45 minutes, or 5:45. Subtract from the ending time.

15:30 − 5:45 = 9:45 a.m.

Subtract 1 hour for lunch and two 20-minute breaks.

9:45 − 1:40 = **8:05 a.m.**

28. C) Total points = 300 (100 for the midterm and 200 for the final).

Set up and solve a proportion to determine the minimum number of points to get a 90.

$\frac{90}{100} = \frac{x}{300} \rightarrow x = 270.$

Subtract the midterm grade.

270 − 92 = 178

Divide by 2 since the final is worth double.

178 ÷ 2 = **89**

29. C) There are 6 people running for office.

president = 6 possible candidates; vice president = 5 possible candidates; secretary = 4 possible candidates

Multiply: 6 × 5 × 4 = **120** ways.

30. B) There are 3 screens that can operate for 10 hours.

Each showing takes $1\frac{1}{2}$ hours plus $\frac{1}{2}$ hour for cleaning = 2 hours total.

Divide: 10 ÷ 2 = 5.

Multiply by the number of screens.

5 × 3 = **15**

31. C) There are 7 seats and 9 people playing.

There is a 7 out of 9 chance or **78%** chance a person is not eliminated.

32. B) Change the percentage to a decimal.

40% = 0.4

Multiply the decimal by the whole (number of voters) to find the part (number of votes for Pauline).

175 × 0.4 = **70**

33. B) Let x = the number of people to attend the party.

$4x + 6 = 50$

Solve for x.

$4x + 6 - 6 = 50 - 6$

$4x = 44$

$x = \mathbf{11}$

34. C) Find the percent change.

$\frac{\text{original} - \text{new}}{\text{original}} \rightarrow \frac{92 - 88}{92} = 0.0435$

Convert to a percent.

4.35% is **between 4 and 5%**.

35. C) Find the number of combinations.

4 meats × 3 cheeses × 2 breads × 4 condiments = **96** different sandwiches.

36. B) Multiply the car's speed by the time traveled to find the distance.

$1.5(65) = 97.5$ miles

$2.5(50) = 125$ miles

$97.5 + 125 = \mathbf{222.5\ miles}$

37. C) Subtract the amount used from the original yards.

$6 - 4\frac{5}{8} \rightarrow 5\frac{8}{8} - 4\frac{5}{8} = \mathbf{1\frac{3}{8}\ yd}$

38. D) Find the daily distance by adding $\frac{1}{4}$ mile to each day.

Day	Monday	Tuesday	Wednesday	Thursday	Friday
Distance	$3\frac{1}{2}$	$3\frac{1}{2} + \frac{1}{4} = 3\frac{3}{4}$	$3\frac{3}{4} + \frac{1}{4} = 4$	$4 + \frac{1}{4} = 4\frac{1}{4}$	$4\frac{1}{4} + \frac{1}{4} = 4\frac{1}{2}$

Add each daily distance to find the total.

$3\frac{2}{4} + 3\frac{3}{4} + 4 + 4\frac{1}{4} + 4\frac{2}{4} =$

$18\frac{8}{4} \rightarrow 18 + 2 = \mathbf{20}$

39. A) Find the amount of sugar the patient will need to cut from his diet.

part = whole × percent

$40 \times 0.25 = 10$

Subtract this amount from the initial value.

$40 - 10 = \mathbf{30\ grams}$

40. D) Add the lengths of the pipe pieces.

$26.5 + 18.9 + 35.1 = \mathbf{80.5\ in}$

41. D) $-4x + 2 = -34$

Isolate x by subtracting two from each side.

$-4x = -36$

Divide by -4.

$x = \mathbf{9}$

42. A) Multiply the monthly payment by the number of months; $158x$.

Subtract from the total bill; **1896 − 158x**.

43. B) Use dimensional analysis to determine the length of time.

$4500\ \text{words} \times \frac{1\ \text{minute}}{45\ \text{words}} =$

100 minutes

44. B) Mean represents the average score. Determine how many points need to be added to 75 to get 81.

$75 + x = 81$

$x = \mathbf{6}$

45. C) Write a proportion and solve.

$$\frac{1 \text{ inch}}{25 \text{ miles}} = \frac{x}{125 \text{ miles}}$$

Cross multiply.

$25x = 125$

$x = \mathbf{5}$

46. C) A light cycle lasts $2\frac{1}{2}$ minutes and Martin is waiting $7\frac{1}{2}$ minutes.

Divide to determine how many cycles.

$7.5 \div 2.5 = 3$.

If each cycle lets 12 cars proceed, the most cycles he waits is 3.

Multiply the number of cars in each cycle: $2(12) = 24$ and $3(12) = 36$.

The only answer between these values is **30**.

47. B) Let $x =$ the number of desktops sold.

The store sold three times as many laptops as desktops.

Let $3x =$ number of laptops.

The number of laptops plus the number of desktops is 56.

$x + 3x = 56$

$4x = 56$

$x = 14$

There were 14 desktops sold and $14(3) = 42$ laptops sold.

Subtract to find how many more laptops than desktops sold.

$42 - 14 = \mathbf{28}$

ISEE Essay

PROMPT

Topic: Driving Age: Is Sixteen Too Young?

Prompt: Some people think the driving age should be raised to eighteen because teenage drivers are inexperienced, easily distracted, and have more accidents. However, teenagers need cars in many parts of the United States for transportation. Write an essay where you express your opinion on this issue. Use examples to support your point of view.

SAMPLE RESPONSE

Some people think states should change the driving age for teens, raising it by one or even two years. Young drivers are inexperienced and could harm themselves and others. But what about the parents and families who depend on teen drivers? Many teenagers need cars to help their families. States should keep the driving age where it is, and use special programs to ensure safety.

Teenagers need to be able to drive. Some teens provide income by working a part-time job that they might need a car for. Their families depend on that income. In addition, many teenagers live in places where they need cars to get to and from school. They may take their younger siblings or neighbors to school or to other activities. Plenty of teens help out their parents by taking younger siblings or elderly relatives who cannot drive to activities, doctors' appointments, and other important places while parents are at work. By raising the driving age, the children and other non-drivers who depend on these teens will suffer.

States should help teen drivers be safer drivers. Just raising the driving age will not make young drivers better drivers. Some states already have graduated licensing and improved driver's education courses for teenagers. These programs reduce injuries and accidents. These states have stricter requirements for teen drivers. As drivers get more experienced, the rules get more relaxed. States could also increase the amount of supervised driving time teens must complete, and limit the number of passengers a teen may carry. All these ideas could help improve a young driver's skills on the road.

Keeping teenagers off the road will inconvenience families and create unnecessary problems for communities. Instead of forbidding teenagers from driving, we should try to help them become better drivers.

CHAPTER SIX
Practice Test Two

Verbal Reasoning
SYNONYMS

Directions: Find the synonym or the word closest in meaning.

1. TRANSIENT
    A) repetitive
    B) severe
    C) extreme
    D) temporary

2. INCOMPATIBLE
    A) friendly
    B) cooperative
    C) mismatched
    D) talkative

3. TRANSMIT
    A) treat
    B) study
    C) pass on
    D) eliminate

4. VOID
    A) ease
    B) strengthen
    C) empty
    D) feel

5. THERAPEUTIC
    A) healing
    B) prescribed
    C) systemic
    D) targeted

6. DISCREET
    A) careful
    B) accurate
    C) loud
    D) exact

7. RECURRENCE
    A) cure
    B) return
    C) resolution
    D) suppression

8. LATENT
    A) obvious
    B) lasting
    C) hidden
    D) misunderstood

9. ANOMALY
   A) crime
   B) mistake
   C) irregularity
   D) improvement

10. IMMINENT
    A) delayed
    B) avoidable
    C) fatal
    D) impending

11. INNOCUOUS
    A) glamorous
    B) healthy
    C) harmless
    D) worrisome

12. MALIGNANT
    A) harmful
    B) mobile
    C) growing
    D) large

13. INGESTING
    A) swallowing
    B) holding
    C) measuring
    D) processing

14. NEXUS
    A) space
    B) source
    C) conduit
    D) center

15. INTACT
    A) overactive
    B) inflamed
    C) ruptured
    D) functional

16. OCCLUDE
    A) obstruct
    B) promote
    C) damage
    D) sustain

17. POSTERIOR
    A) rear
    B) front
    C) side
    D) top

18. IMPAIR
    A) concentrate
    B) allow
    C) increase
    D) weaken

19. CHRONIC
    A) difficult
    B) periodic
    C) secondary
    D) persistent

20. LETHARGIC
    A) energized
    B) curious
    C) tired
    D) confused

SINGLE-WORD RESPONSE

Directions: Choose the word that best completes the sentence.

1. Be sure to be extra _____ when taking care of your friend's cat; she is counting on you to make sure the cat has plenty of food, water, and love.
   - A) attentive
   - B) friendly
   - C) careful
   - D) harmonious

2. The wicked witch was _____ from the area and was told never to return again.
   - A) invited
   - B) floundered
   - C) banished
   - D) escaped

3. After the subway stopped suddenly at the platform, there was a loud _____ coming from the station as workers rushed by.
   - A) commotion
   - B) quietude
   - C) stillness
   - D) tranquility

4. I always wondered what would have happened if Jack hadn't broken the top of his head or _____ and instead had simply tumbled down the hill with Jill.
   - A) elbow
   - B) cap
   - C) crown
   - D) jaw

5. The lightning bugs gave off an _____ glow in the evening.
   - A) angry
   - B) energetic
   - C) overwhelming
   - D) iridescent

6. By Saturday, the snow and wind is expected to _____; it should be sunny and warm on Sunday.
   - A) multiply
   - B) diminish
   - C) duplicate
   - D) increase

7. Clara hoped to _____ the nasty rumor by passing out cupcakes and compliments to everyone who had called her mean.
   - A) exaggerate
   - B) attract
   - C) dispel
   - D) start

8. The mother was _____ with her son when he refused to get off of his electronics.
   - A) happy
   - B) placated
   - C) exasperated
   - D) energized

Practice Test Two 115

9. The runner started to _____ and lost her energy during the marathon; as a result, she walked the rest of the way.
   A) rile
   B) falter
   C) rally
   D) stabilize

10. The athletes had a _____ twelve-hour workout; they were exhausted at the end of the day.
    A) grueling
    B) troublesome
    C) moderate
    D) sufficient

11. Even though the desert doesn't seem like an ideal place for _____, many animals and insects live there.
    A) racing
    B) dehydration
    C) water
    D) habitation

12. As the sirens blared warning us of an _____ tornado, we quickly took shelter in a nearby cellar.
    A) overnight
    B) outlying
    C) ebbing
    D) impending

13. The two guinea pigs _____ at me, making a lot of noise, until I gave them some hay.
    A) laughed
    B) jabbered
    C) looked
    D) gazed

14. The horse had a long tooth _____ out from its mouth.
    A) dissipating
    B) upright
    C) suspending
    D) jutting

15. As I walked by the house, the smell of apple pie _____ through the air and made me salivate.
    A) wafted
    B) waited
    C) heated
    D) wavered

DOUBLE-WORD RESPONSE

Directions: Choose the pair of words that best completes the sentence.

1. It was clear from the vocabulary used that the essay was _____ and not an _____ piece of writing.
   A) plagiarized… original
   B) commonplace… avoidable
   C) purloined… unoriginal
   D) legal… exemplar

2. It would be very _____ of you to bring an extra pair of clothes when you go camping, just in case you _____ in the lake.
   A) cautious… cascade
   B) silly… swim
   C) reckless… jump
   D) prudent… plummet

116 ISEE Upper Level Test Prep

3. At the end of the movie, the robotic aliens _____ the planet, causing all _____ life to disappear.
   A) created... inanimate
   B) annihilated... dead
   C) obliterated... sentient
   D) abolished... unresponsive

4. Let's settle this _____ and peacefully; there's no reason for us to continue our _____.
   A) tranquilly... ambiguity
   B) amicably... dispute
   C) disagreeably... brutality
   D) aggressively... intenseness

5. We all waited inside for the rain to _____ so that we could go outside and _____ in the sunshine.
   A) replicate... thrive
   B) proliferate... gather
   C) abate... revel
   D) rise... celebrate

Answer Key
SYNONYMS

1. **D)** *Transient* means temporary or lasting for only a short period of time.

2. **C)** *Incompatible* means unable to work together or mismatched.

3. **C)** To *transmit* something is to send it or pass it on.

4. **C)** *Void* can be a noun or a verb, meaning emptiness, to empty, or to evacuate.

5. **A)** *Therapeutic* means having a beneficial or healing effect.

6. **A)** *Discreet* means considerate or careful to avoid causing offense or injury.

7. **B)** When something *recurs*, it "returns" or "appears again." *Recurrence* is the noun form of the verb *recur*.

8. **C)** *Latent* means hidden or dormant.

9. **C)** An *anomaly* is a deviation from the norm or an irregularity.

10. **D)** *Imminent* means about to happen.

11. **C)** *Innocuous* takes its origins from the Latin *in–*, meaning "not," and *nocuus*, meaning "injurious." Hence, the word means not injurious or not harmful.

12. **A)** The prefix of *malignant* is *mal–*, meaning bad or evil. "Malignant" means harmful.

13. **A)** *Ingesting* something means to take into the body for digestion.

14. **D)** *Nexus* means a connection between two or more things, or the central or most important place.

15. **D)** *Intact* means whole or uninjured.

16. **A)** *Occlude* means to shut in or out; to close; obstruct passage.

17. **A)** *Posterior* refers to any location in the rear or the back.

18. **D)** *Impair* means to weaken or damage.

19. **D)** *Chronic* means persistent or recurring over a long period of time.

20. **C)** *Lethargic* means sluggish, sleepy, or tired.

SINGLE-WORD RESPONSE

1. **A)** *Attentive* means to pay close attention to.

2. **C)** To *banish* means to kick out; the witch was kicked out or banished from the area—never to return again.

3. **A)** *Commotion* means uproar or disturbance.

4. **C)** The top of a person's head is also called a *crown*.

5. **D)** *Iridescent* means dazzling, shimmering, or lustrous.

6. **B)** *Diminish* means to reduce or weaken. Because it is expected to be sunny and warm the following day, the snow and wind will lessen, or diminish.

7. **C)** To *dispel* means to drive out or chase away or get rid of.

8. **C)** *Exasperated* means frustrated, annoyed, or irritated.

9. **B)** *Falter* means to hesitate, weaken, or pause.

10. **A)** *Grueling* means tough, arduous, and tiring.

11. **D)** *Habitation* means abode or home. Animals and insects make their homes or habitats in the desert.

12. **D)** *Impending* means imminent, just around the corner, or looming.

13. **B)** *Jabbered* means to chatter, talk, or make lots of noise.

14. **D)** *Jutting* means sticking out or protruding.

15. **A)** *Wafted* refers to when a scent drifts, floats, or is carried through the air.

DOUBLE-WORD RESPONSE

1. **A)** *Plagiarized* means stolen or copied without permission; *original* means unique, new, or innovative.

2. **D)** *Prudent* means practical or sensible; *plummet* means to fall.

3. **C)** *Obliterated* means completely destroyed; *sentient* means conscious or aware.

4. **B)** *Amicably* means harmoniously or in a friendly manner; a *dispute* is an argument or fight.

5. **C)** *Abate* means to end or stop; *revel* means to bask in or delight.

Quantitative Reasoning

1.

Column A	Column B
The slope of the line $y = -7x$	The slope perpendicular to the line $y = \frac{1}{7}x$

- **A)** The quantity in Column A is greater.
- **B)** The quantity in Column B is greater.
- **C)** The two quantities are equal.
- **D)** The relationship cannot be determined from the information given.

2.

Column A	Column B
The number of even prime numbers between 1 and 1000	The number of odd prime numbers between 1 and 1000

- **A)** The quantity in Column A is greater.
- **B)** The quantity in Column B is greater.
- **C)** The two quantities are equal.
- **D)** The relationship cannot be determined from the information given.

3. Most pizzerias determine the size of their pizzas by their diameter.

Column A	Column B
The area of one 16-inch circle	The area of two 8-inch circles

- **A)** The quantity in Column A is greater.
- **B)** The quantity in Column B is greater.
- **C)** The two quantities are equal.
- **D)** The relationship cannot be determined from the information given.

4. Solve with the fact that $x > 1$, $y > 1$, and $z < 0$

Column A	Column B
$\dfrac{(x^3 \times x^2)}{(x \times y^2 \times z^{12})0}$	x^{-2}

- **A)** The quantity in Column A is greater.
- **B)** The quantity in Column B is greater.
- **C)** The two quantities are equal.
- **D)** The relationship cannot be determined from the information given.

5.

Column A	Column B
The number of days in two weeks	The number of hours in $\frac{2}{3}$ of a day

- **A)** The quantity in Column A is greater.
- **B)** The quantity in Column B is greater.
- **C)** The two quantities are equal.
- **D)** The relationship cannot be determined from the information given.

6. For $0 \leq x \leq 1$

Column A	Column B
x^2	x^4

- **A)** The quantity in Column A is greater.
- **B)** The quantity in Column B is greater.
- **C)** The two quantities are equal.
- **D)** The relationship cannot be determined from the information given.

7.

Column A	Column B
The number of sides in a kite	The number of sides in a trapezoid

- **A)** The quantity in Column A is greater.
- **B)** The quantity in Column B is greater.
- **C)** The two quantities are equal.
- **D)** The relationship cannot be determined from the information given.

8. Cynthia drives an average of 55 miles per hour. Heather drives an average of 60 miles per hour.

Column A	Column B
The distance driven by Cynthia	The distance driven by Heather

- **A)** The quantity in Column A is greater.
- **B)** The quantity in Column B is greater.
- **C)** The two quantities are equal.
- **D)** The relationship cannot be determined from the information given.

9. Triangles *ABC* and *DFG* are equiangular.

Column A	Column B
The area of triangle *ABC*	The area of triangle *DFG*

- **A)** The quantity in Column A is greater.
- **B)** The quantity in Column B is greater.
- **C)** The two quantities are equal.
- **D)** The relationship cannot be determined from the information given.

10.

Column A	Column B
0	$\dfrac{x^3}{(x)(x^4)(x^{-2})}$

A) The quantity in Column A is greater.
B) The quantity in Column B is greater.
C) The two quantities are equal.
D) The relationship cannot be determined from the information given.

11. A radio station's playlist consists of 20% rap songs, 30% country songs, 40% rock songs, and 10% easy listening.

Column A	Column B
The probability the station will not play two country songs in succession	50%

A) The quantity in Column A is greater.
B) The quantity in Column B is greater.
C) The two quantities are equal.
D) The relationship cannot be determined from the information given.

12.

Column A	Column B
The number of pairs of parallel sides of a regular octagon	The number of sides of a trapezoid

A) The quantity in Column A is greater.
B) The quantity in Column B is greater.
C) The two quantities are equal.
D) The relationship cannot be determined from the information given.

13. Two cylinders have the same base. Cylinder A has a height of x and Cylinder B has a height of 2x. What is true regarding the relationship between the two cylinders? (The formula for the surface area of a cylinder is SA = $2\pi rh + 2\pi r^2$, and the formula for the volume of a cylinder is V = $\pi r^2 h$.)
    A) Cylinder A's surface area is $\frac{1}{2}$ that of Cylinder B.
    B) Cylinder B's surface area is $\frac{1}{2}$ that of Cylinder A.
    C) Cylinder A has a volume $\frac{1}{2}$ that of Cylinder B.
    D) Cylinder B has a volume $\frac{1}{2}$ that of Cylinder A.

14. Marcus got the highest score on a science test, a 96. If his teacher tells the class the range of the test scores was 35, what does that mean?
    A) Thirty-five students took the test.
    B) The average test score was a 61.
    C) The middle test score was a 61.
    D) The lowest test score was a 61.

15. Lydia draws a triangle on a piece of paper. She measures two of the angles to be 23 degrees and 37 degrees. What kind of triangle did she draw?
    A) Acute
    B) Equilateral
    C) Obtuse
    D) Right

16. If $x + y$ is an odd number, which of the following must be true?
    A) Both x and y must be odd numbers.
    B) Neither x nor y can equal 0.
    C) Either x or y is odd, while the other is even.
    D) The product of x and y is odd.

17. A vending machine contains 12 types of snacks. Some snacks are salty, and some snacks are sweet. The ratio of sweet snacks to salty snacks is 1:3. How many types of sweet snacks are in the vending machine?
    A) 1
    B) 3
    C) 4
    D) 12

18. Which of the following equations describes the linear relationship between x and y shown in the table?

X	Y
3	11
5	15
8	21

    A) $y = 2x + 5$
    B) $y = 5x + 5$
    C) $y = 4x + 5$
    D) $y = 3x + 5$

19. Which of the following equations correctly solves the word problem given below?

> At a party, 6 girls and 9 boys each order a hot dog for $2 each. How much money was spent for hot dogs?

A) $2 \times 6 + 9 = \$21$
B) $2 + 6 + 9 = \$17$
C) $2 \times (6 + 9) = \$30$
D) $2 \times 6 \times 9 = \$108$

20. A whole number is divided by 3. Which of the following CANNOT be the remainder?

A) 0
B) 1
C) 2
D) 3

21. Which of the following is listed in order from least to greatest?

A) $-0.95, 0, \frac{2}{5}, 0.35, \frac{3}{4}$
B) $-1, -\frac{1}{10}, -0.11, \frac{5}{6}, 0.75$
C) $-\frac{3}{4}, -0.2, 0, \frac{2}{3}, 0.55$
D) $-1.1, -\frac{4}{5}, -0.13, 0.7, \frac{9}{11}$

22. Which of the following is closest in value to $129{,}113 + 34{,}602$?

A) 162,000
B) 163,000
C) 164,000
D) 165,000

23. Which expression has only prime factors of 3, 5, and 11?

A) 66×108
B) 15×99
C) 42×29
D) 28×350

24. Which inequality is represented by the following graph?

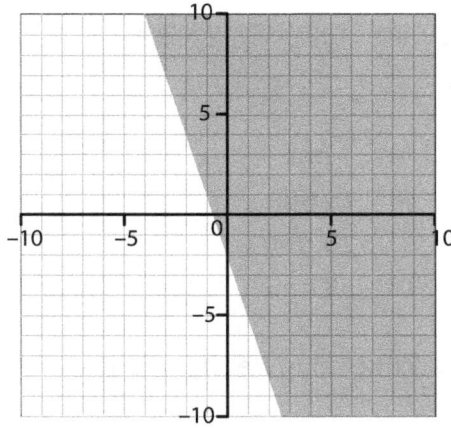

A) $y \geq -3x - 2$
B) $y \geq 3x - 2$
C) $y > -3x - 2$
D) $y \leq -3x - 2$

25. Valerie receives a base salary of $740 a week for working 40 hours. For every extra hour she works, she is paid at a rate of $27.75 per hour. If Valerie works t hours in a week, which of the following equations represents the amount of money, A, she will receive?

A) $A = 740 + 27.75(t - 40)$
B) $A = 740 + 27.75(40 - t)$
C) $A = 27.75t - 740$
D) $A = 27.75t + 740$

26. Identify the missing number in the sequence: 1, ___, 5, 7, 9, ...

A) 0
B) 2
C) 3
D) 4

27. How much longer is line segment MN than line segment KL?

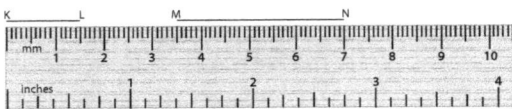

- A) 2 mm
- B) 15 mm
- C) 20 mm
- D) 55 mm

28. Which number has the least value?
- A) 0.305
- B) 0.035
- C) 0.35
- D) 0.3

29. Which graph shows the solution to $y = 2x + 1$?

A)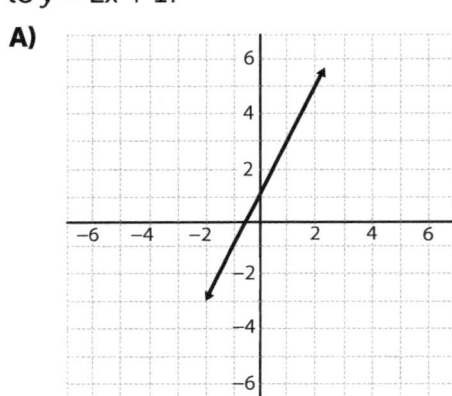

B)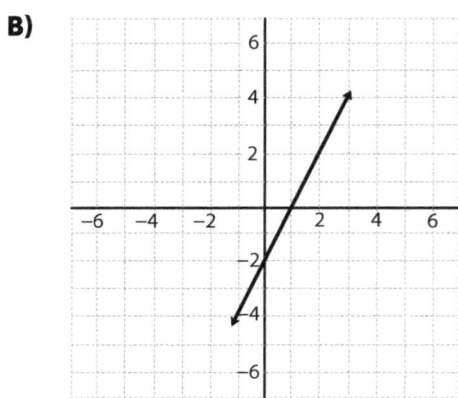

C)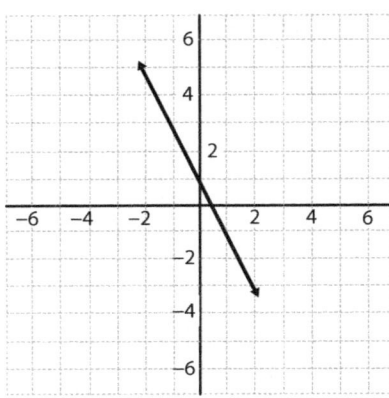

D)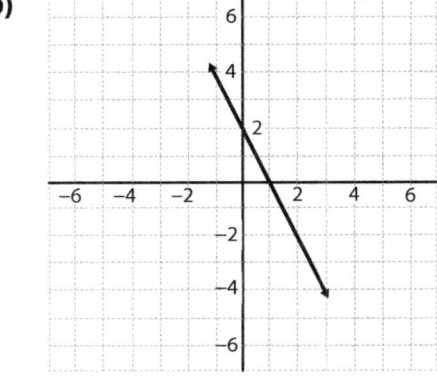

30. The graph below shows the number of months that Chicago, New York, and Houston had less than 3 inches of rain from 2009 to 2015.

New York had the fewest months with less than 3 inches of rain in every year except:
- A) 2012
- B) 2013
- C) 2014
- D) 2015

Practice Test Two 125

31. What is the greatest common factor of 45 and 22?
  A) 1
  B) 2
  C) 9
  D) 11

32. Which of the following operations is equivalent to dividing by 100?
  A) multiplying by $\frac{1}{100}$
  B) adding (−100)
  C) dividing by $\frac{1}{100}$
  D) multiplying by 0.001

33. Which of the following is equivalent to the term 5n for all values of n?
  A) $5n^5 - n^4$
  B) $3n + 2n$
  C) n^5
  D) $5 + n$

34. What is the median of all the even integers greater than 10 and less than 25?
  A) 14
  B) 16
  C) 18
  D) 20

35. How many digits are in the number four hundred twenty-three and nine thousandths?
  A) 4
  B) 5
  C) 6
  D) 7

36. Which of the following values is between $\frac{3}{4}$ and $\frac{9}{10}$?
  A) 0.92
  B) 0.55
  C) 0.80
  D) 0.72

37. Which of the following is equivalent to 1 meter?
  A) 5280 ft
  B) 0.001 km
  C) 1000 cm
  D) 3 ft

Answer Key

1. **C)** Slope-intercept form, $y = mx + b$, with m = slope and b = y-intercept.

   Columxn A: the slope is −7.

   Column B: the slope is perpendicular to $\frac{1}{7}$.

   Perpendicular slopes are negative reciprocals. Therefore, **the two quantities are equal**.

2. **B)** A prime number is divisible only by 1 and itself.

   Column A: All even numbers greater than 2 are divisible by 2. There is only one even prime number, which is 2.

   Column B: There are numerous prime numbers between 1 and 1000 (167 to be exact).

   The quantity in Column B is greater.

3. **A)** Determine the area of the pizzas given in each column.

   Column A: A 16-inch pizza will have a radius of 8 inches.

   $A = \pi r^2 \rightarrow A = \pi(8)^2 \rightarrow 64\pi$

   Column B: An 8-inch pizza will have a radius of 4 inches.

   $A = \pi r^2 \rightarrow A = \pi(4)^2 \rightarrow 16\pi \times 2$ pizzas $= 32\pi$

   The quantity in Column A is greater.

4. **A)** Column A: The fraction is being raised to the power of 0. Any number raised to the power of 0 is equal to 1.

   Column B: Since x is greater than 1, the value of x^{-2} is equivalent to $\frac{1}{x^2}$. The value of Column B is between 0 and 1.

   The quantity of Column A is greater.

5. **B)** Column A: 2 weeks = 14 days

   Column B: The number of hours in $\frac{2}{3}$ of a day is $\frac{2}{3} \times 24 = 16$ hours.

   The quantity in Column B is greater.

6. **D)** If x is equal to 0 or 1, the two quantities would be equal. If the value of x is between 0 and 1, then in most cases, the quantity in Column A is greater. There is not enough information, so **the relationship cannot be determined from the information given**.

7. **C)** Both kites and trapezoids are quadrilaterals, which have 4 sides. **The two quantities are equal.**

8. **D)** The speeds are given, but the time spent driving is not given. **The relationship cannot be determined from the information given.**

9. **D)** *Equiangular* means the two triangles each have the same angle measurement. The triangles have the same angle measures and would therefore be similar. However, the length of the triangles is not given. **The relationship cannot be determined from the information given.**

10. **B)** In Column B, simplify the denominator by adding exponents. $1 + 4 + (-2) = 3$.

    This gives $\frac{x^3}{x^3}$, which simplifies to 1. **The quantity in Column B is greater.**

Practice Test Two

11. **B)** The probability a station plays country music = 30%.

    The probability it would not play country music = 70%.

    The probability the station would not play two country songs in succession:

    70% × 70% or 0.7 × 0.7 = 0.49 → 49%

    49% < 50%

    The quantity in Column B is greater.

12. **C)** An octagon has 8 sides. A regular octagon will have four pairs of parallel sides. A trapezoid is a quadrilateral, which has 4 sides. **The two quantities are equal.**

13. **C)** Cylinder A: Surface Area → $SA = 2\pi rx + 2\pi r^2$; Volume → $V = \pi r^2 x$.

    Cylinder B: Surface Area → $SA = 4\pi rx + 2\pi r^2$; Volume → $V = 2\pi r^2 x$.

    Cylinder A has half the volume of Cylinder B.

14. **D)** Marcus scored the highest on a test with a 96. The range is 35 which means the spread of scores from lowest to highest is 35 points. The lowest test score would be 96 − 35 = **61**.

15. **C)** Two angles are 23 + 37 = 60 degrees.

    All triangles have a sum of 180 degrees.

    Third angle: 180 − 60 = 120 degrees.

    Since 120 degrees is an obtuse angle, her triangle must be **obtuse**.

16. **C)** Odd + odd = even → Eliminate choice A.

    Either x or y can equal 0, but they do not necessarily have to be. → Eliminate choice B.

    Odd × even = even → Eliminate choice D.

    For the sum of two numbers to be odd, one number must be odd and the other even. → Choice **C** is correct.

17. **B)** Total snacks = 12.

    The numbers on both sides of the ratio must equal 12. If both sides of the ratio are multiplied by 3, the ratio of salty to sweet would be 3:9.

    3 sweet snacks + 9 salty snacks = 12 total snacks.

18. **A)** Find the slope using the values in the table.
    $$m = \frac{y_2 - y_1}{x_2 - x_1} = \frac{15 - 11}{5 - 3} = \frac{4}{2} = 2$$
    Alternatively, substitute an ordered pair from the table into the equations.

    y = 2x + 5

    11 = 2(3) + 5

    11 = 11

19. **C)** The total number of children is described within the parentheses. Since each hot dog costs $2, that total is multiplied by 2.

    2 × (6 + 9) = $30

20. **D)** The remainder of a division problem must be less than the divisor. The remainder cannot be **3**.

21. **D)** Write each value in decimal form and compare.

    A) −0.95 < 0 < 0.4 < 0.35 < 0.75 FALSE

B) $-1 < -0.1 < -0.11 < 0.8\overline{3} \le 0.75$
FALSE

C) $-0.75 < -0.2 < 0 < 0.\overline{6} \le 0.55$
FALSE

D) $-1.1 < -0.8 < -0.13 < 0.7 < 0.\overline{81}$ TRUE

22. C) Round each value to the nearest thousand.

129,113 ≈ 129,000

34,602 ≈ 35,000

Add.

129,000 + 35,000 = **164,000**

23. B) The numbers 66, 42, and 28 are all even numbers. Answer choices A, B, and C can all be divisible by 2. The expressions **15 × 99** has factors of 3, 5, and 11.

24. A) Graphing $y = -3x - 2$ gives a line with a slope of -3 and a y-intercept of -2. Because the symbol is greater than or equal to ($\ge$), the line is solid and the graph is shaded above the line; **$y \ge -3x - 2$**.

25. A) Valerie will receive her base pay plus 27.75 for every hour she worked in addition to 40 hours.

A = base pay + 27.75 × extra hours

$A = 740 + 27.75(t - 40)$

26. C) The sequence is formed by adding 2 to the previous term; $1 + 2 = $ **3**.

27. C) Line segment MN begins at 35 mm and ends at 70 mm, so $70 - 35 = 35$ mm.

The length of line segment KL is 15 mm.

Find the difference.

35 mm − 15 mm = **20 mm**.

28. B) Compare decimals from left to right. Three of the numbers have a 3 in the tenths place, while one has a zero. The number with the least value is **0.035**.

29. A) Use a table to find coordinates of $y = 2x + 1$.

x	y
0	1
1	3
2	5

Plot the coordinates (0, 1), (1, 3), and (2, 5). Connect the points with a line. **The graph is choice A.**

30. A) In **2012,** New York had more months with less than 3 inches of rain than either Chicago or Houston.

31. A) Find the prime factorization of each number.

$45 = 3 \times 3 \times 5$

$22 = 2 \times 11$

The two numbers have no prime factors in common. Because 1 is a factor of every number, their greatest common factor is **1**.

32. A) $n \div 100 = \frac{n}{100}$

$n \times \frac{1}{100} = \frac{n}{100}$

Dividing by 100 produces the same result as **multiplying by $\frac{1}{100}$**.

33. B) Combine like terms.

$5n =$ **$3n + 2n$**

34. C) List all the even integers greater than 10 and less than 25 in ascending order. The median is the value in the middle.

12, 14, 16, **18**, 20, 22, 24

35. **C)** Four hundred twenty-three and nine thousandths is written as 423.009. It has **6 digits.**

36. **C)** Convert each fraction to a decimal.

    $\frac{3}{4} = 0.75$

    $\frac{9}{10} = 0.90$

    The value **0.80** is between 0.75 and 0.90.

37. **B)** There are 1000 meters in 1 kilometer, so 1 meter = **0.001 km**.

Reading Comprehension

The most important part of brewing coffee is getting the right water. Choose a water that you think has a nice, neutral flavor. Anything with too many minerals or contaminants will change the flavor of the coffee, and water with too few minerals won't do a good job of extracting the flavor from the coffee beans. Water should be heated to between 195 and 205 degrees Fahrenheit. Boiling water (212 degrees Fahrenheit) will burn the beans and give your coffee a scorched flavor.

While the water is heating, grind your beans. Remember, the fresher the grind, the fresher the flavor of the coffee. The number of beans is entirely dependent on your personal taste. Obviously, more beans will result in a more robust flavor, while fewer beans will give your coffee a subtler taste. The texture of the grind should be not too fine (which can lead to bitter coffee) or too large (which can lead to weak coffee).

Once the beans are ground and the water has reached the perfect temperature, you're ready to brew. A French press (which we recommend) allows you to control brewing time and provide a thorough brew. Pour the grounds into the press, and then pour the hot water over the grounds and let them steep. The brew shouldn't require more than five minutes, although you can leave it longer if you like your coffee a bit harsher. Finally, use the plunger to remove the grounds and pour.

1. According to the passage, if the texture of the bean grind is too large, how will the coffee taste?
   A) scorched
   B) bitter
   C) weak
   D) fresh

2. What does the word *steep* most likely mean in this passage?
   A) boil
   B) taste
   C) grind
   D) soak

3. Which detail best supports the claim that choosing the right water when brewing coffee is important?
   A) Water with too many minerals or contaminants will change the flavor of the coffee.
   B) While the water is heating, grind your beans.
   C) Boiling water will burn the beans and give your coffee a scorched flavor.
   D) Pour the hot water over the grounds and let them steep.

4. Which of the following statements is a fact?
   A) The most important part of brewing coffee is getting the right water.
   B) Those of you who like your coffee a bit harsher can leave it longer.
   C) The fresher the grind, the fresher the flavor of the coffee.
   D) The French press allows you to control brewing time and provide a thorough brew.

5. What conclusion can be made about brewing coffee based on the passage?
   A) Using a French press to brew coffee is an essential step to making quality coffee.
   B) Brewing a quality cup of coffee is an intricate process that requires attention to detail.
   C) Grinding beans to a fine texture will result in weak coffee.
   D) Beans will taste the same regardless of when they are ground.

Influenza (also called the flu) has historically been one of the most common, and deadliest, human infections. While many people who contract the virus will recover, many others will not. Over the past 150 years, tens of millions of people have died from the flu, and millions more have been left with lingering complications such as secondary infections.

Although it's a common disease, the flu is not actually highly infectious, meaning it's relatively difficult to contract. The flu can only be transmitted when individuals come into direct contact with bodily fluids of people infected with the flu or when they are exposed to <u>expelled</u> aerosol particles (which result from coughing and sneezing). Because the viruses can only travel short distances as aerosol particles and die within a few hours on hard surfaces, the virus can be contained with fairly simple health measures like hand washing and face masks.

However, the spread of the flu can only be contained when people are aware such measures need to be taken. One of the reasons the flu has historically been so deadly is the amount of time between when people become infectious and when they develop symptoms. Viral shedding—the process by which the body releases viruses that have been successfully reproducing during the infection—takes place two days after infection, while symptoms do not usually develop until the third day of infection. Thus, infected individuals have at least twenty-four hours in which they may unknowingly infect others.

6. The act of releasing viruses that have been reproducing is called
   A) contagious.
   B) viral shedding.
   C) influenza.
   D) aerosol particles.

7. What is the primary purpose of the passage?
   A) to persuade readers to cover their mouths when they cough
   B) to argue in favor of the flu vaccine
   C) to explain why the flu is so common
   D) to inform readers of the symptoms of the flu so it can be identified

8. In this passage, what does the word *expelled* most likely mean?
   A) noninfectious
   B) ejected
   C) harmful
   D) hidden

9. Because of the significant amount of time between when people with the flu become infectious and when they develop symptoms,
   A) many infected individuals unknowingly infect others.
   B) millions have been left with lingering complications.
   C) the infection is not highly contagious.
   D) viruses can only travel short distances.

10. According to the passage, which of the following is TRUE about the flu virus?
    A) It can live on hard surfaces for up to two days.
    B) It is highly infectious and easy to spread to others.
    C) It has killed tens of millions in the past 150 years.
    D) It travels long distances as aerosol particles after a sneeze.

The bacteria, fungi, insects, plants, and animals that live together in a habitat have evolved to share a pool of limited resources. They've competed for water, minerals, nutrients, sunlight, and space—sometimes for thousands or even millions of years. As these communities have evolved, the species in them have developed complex, long-term interspecies interactions known as symbiotic relationships.

Ecologists characterize these interactions based on whether each party benefits. In mutualism, both individuals benefit, while in synnecrosis, both organisms are harmed. A relationship where one individual benefits and the other is harmed is known as parasitism. Examples of these relationships can easily be seen in any ecosystem. Pollination, for example, is mutualistic—pollinators get nutrients from the flower, and the plant is able to reproduce—while tapeworms, which steal nutrients from their host, are parasitic.

There's yet another class of symbiosis that is controversial among scientists. As it's long been defined, commensalism is a relationship where one species benefits and the other is unaffected. But is it possible for two species to interact and one remain completely unaffected? Often, relationships described as commensal include one species that feeds on another species' leftovers; remoras, for instance, attach themselves to sharks and eat the food particles sharks leave behind. It might seem like the shark gets nothing from the relationship, but a closer look shows that sharks in fact benefit from remoras, which clean the sharks' skin and remove parasites. In fact, many scientists claim that relationships currently described as commensal are just mutualistic or parasitic in ways that haven't been discovered yet.

11. An organism involved in synnecrosis will
    A) benefit from the relationship.
    B) be unaffected by the relationship.
    C) be harmed by the relationship.
    D) be harmed only if the other benefits.

12. According to the passage, why is commensalism different from the other types of symbiotic relationships?
    A) It is a characterization of symbiotic relationships that is widely accepted by scientists.
    B) Only one organism in this type of symbiotic relationship benefits.
    C) At least one organism is believed to be unaffected by the symbiotic relationship.
    D) It is a type of complex, long-term interspecies interaction.

13. In pollination,
    A) both organisms benefit.
    B) both organisms are harmed.
    C) one organism benefits and the other is harmed.
    D) one organism benefits and the other is unaffected.

14. What is the topic of this passage?
    A) types of commensalism
    B) controversies in science
    C) the dangers of cohabitation
    D) symbiotic relationships

15. One example of a symbiotic relationship is algae and the spider crab. Algae live on the spider crab's back, allowing the algae a place to live and the crab camouflage to hide from predators. What type of relationship is this?
    A) mutualism
    B) synnecrosis
    C) parasitism
    D) commensalism

In a remote nature preserve in northeastern Siberia, scientists are attempting to re-create the subarctic steppe grassland ecosystem that flourished there during the last Ice Age. The area today is dominated by forests, but the lead scientists of the project believe the forested terrain is neither a natural development nor environmentally advantageous. They believe that if they can restore the grassland, they will be able to slow climate change by slowing the thawing of the permafrost that lies beneath the tundra. Key to this undertaking is restoring the wildlife to the region, including wild horses, musk oxen, bison, and yak. Most ambitiously, the scientists hope to <u>revive</u> the wooly mammoth species, which was key in trampling the ground and knocking down the trees, helping to keep the land free for grasses to grow.

16. By slowing the thawing of permafrost, scientists believe they will be able to
    A) bring back the wooly mammoth.
    B) preserve a region of Siberia.
    C) slow global warming.
    D) clear the trees in the forest.

17. Why do the scientists believe that a key task in re-creating the subarctic steppe grassland is to restore wildlife to the region?
    A) Wildlife causes grass to grow by fertilizing the soil.
    B) Wildlife reduces the number of trees in the region.

C) Wildlife speeds the process of climate change and thawing permafrost.
D) Wildlife preserves the forests by playing a vital role in the ecosystem.

18. This paragraph is chiefly concerned with the revitalization of what?
    A) the wooly mammoth
    B) permafrost
    C) grassland
    D) climate

19. Based on the passage, what can be inferred about trees in this region?
    A) They were an important part of the subarctic steppe grassland ecosystem of the last Ice Age.
    B) They must increase in order for scientists to slow the thawing of permafrost.
    C) They ward off wildlife in order to stabilize the climate of this area.
    D) They exist today as a result of human interference with the natural ecosystem.

20. Based on the passage, what does the word *revive* most likely mean?
    A) bring back
    B) get rid of
    C) support
    D) reverse

For thirteen years, a spacecraft called *Cassini* was on an exploratory mission to Saturn. The spacecraft was designed not to return but to end its journey by diving into Saturn's atmosphere. This dramatic ending provided scientists with unprecedented information about Saturn's atmosphere and its magnetic and gravitational fields. First, however, *Cassini* passed Saturn's largest moon, Titan, where it recorded data on Titan's curious methane lakes, gathering information about potential seasons on the planet-sized moon. Then it passed through the unexplored region between Saturn itself and its famous rings. Scientists hope to learn how old the rings are and to directly examine the particles that make them up. *Cassini's* mission ended in 2017, but researchers have new questions for future exploration.

21. In the paragraph, what does the word *unprecedented* most likely mean?
    A) not valuable
    B) unable to understand
    C) not previously known
    D) without logic

22. The paragraph is chiefly concerned with the impact of what?
    A) Saturn's rings
    B) a spacecraft called *Cassini*
    C) Titan's methane lakes
    D) space exploration

23. Based on the passage, which of the following is TRUE about Saturn?

 A) It experiences all four seasons.
 B) It has a strong magnetic field surrounding it.
 C) It is one of the few planets scientists have explored.
 D) It has more than one moon.

24. Based on the passage, we can conclude that before *Cassini's* mission began

 A) a spacecraft had never reached Saturn's atmosphere.
 B) little was known about the region between Saturn and its rings.
 C) the existence of Titan had been unknown to scientists.
 D) scientists had not attempted to study Saturn.

25. Why didn't *Cassini* return to Earth?

 A) It was destroyed by Saturn's rings.
 B) Scientists lost contact with the spacecraft.
 C) The plan for the spacecraft was to never return.
 D) It landed on Titan and continues to record data.

> The Gatling gun, a forerunner of the modern machine gun, was an early rapid-fire spring-loaded, hand-cranked weapon. In 1861, Dr. Richard J. Gatling designed the gun to allow one person to fire many shots quickly. His goal was to reduce the death toll of war by decreasing the number of soldiers needed to fight. The gun consisted of a central shaft surrounded by six rotating barrels. A soldier turned a crank, which rotated the shaft. As each barrel reached a particular point in the cycle, it fired, ejected its spent cartridge, and loaded another. During this process, the barrel cooled down, preparing it to fire again. The Gatling gun was first used in combat by the Union Army during the Civil War. However, each gun was purchased directly by individual commanders. The US Army did not purchase a Gatling gun until 1866.

26. What can be concluded from this passage?

 A) Gatling guns were expensive during the Civil War and still are pricey today.
 B) A soldier was able to fire more shots with the Gatling gun than other guns of its time.
 C) Dr. Richard J. Gatling was a soldier who fought for the Union Army during the Civil War.
 D) The invention of the Gatling gun has led to fewer casualties during wartime.

27. In order for the shaft of the Gatling gun to rotate, a soldier had to

- **A)** pull a trigger.
- **B)** turn a crank.
- **C)** remove the spent cartridge.
- **D)** reload the gun.

28. The passage says that during the Civil War, Gatling guns

- **A)** caused more casualties than any other weapon.
- **B)** led the Union Army to victory against the Confederacy.
- **C)** were purchased by commanders and not the US Army.
- **D)** needed several minutes to cool before firing again.

29. What did Dr. Richard J. Gatling believe?

- **A)** the Gatling gun would reduce the number of soldiers needed in war
- **B)** the Union Army deserved to win the Civil War
- **C)** rapid-fire spring-loaded guns should only be used during wartime
- **D)** the design of the Gatling gun was simple enough for anyone to use

30. What is the topic of this passage?

- **A)** the Civil War
- **B)** the evolution of modern weaponry
- **C)** Dr. Richard J. Gatling
- **D)** an early rapid-fire gun

Hand washing is one of our simplest and most powerful weapons against infection. The idea behind hand washing is deceptively simple. Many illnesses are spread when people touch infected surfaces, such as door handles or other people's hands, and then touch their own eyes, mouths, or noses. So, if pathogens can be removed from the hands before they spread, infections can be prevented. When done correctly, hand washing can prevent the spread of many dangerous bacteria and viruses, including those that cause the flu, the common cold, diarrhea, and many acute respiratory illnesses.

The most basic method of hand washing involves only soap and water. Just twenty seconds of scrubbing with soap and a complete rinsing with water is enough to kill and/or wash away many pathogens. The process doesn't even require warm water—studies have shown that cold water is just as effective at reducing the number of microbes on the hands. Antibacterial soaps are also available, although several studies have shown that simple soap and cold water are just as effective.

In recent years, hand sanitizers have become popular as an alternative to hand washing. These gels, liquids, and foams contain a high concentration of alcohol (usually at least 60 percent) that kills most bacteria and fungi; they can also be effective against some, but not all, viruses. There is a downside to hand sanitizer, however. Because the sanitizer isn't rinsed from hands, it only kills pathogens and does nothing to remove organic matter. So, hands "cleaned" with hand sanitizer may still <u>harbor</u> pathogens. Thus, while hand sanitizer can be helpful in situations where soap and clean water isn't available, a simple hand washing is still the best option.

31. What is the meaning of the word *harbor* in the last paragraph?
  A) to disguise
  B) to hide
  C) to wash away
  D) to give a home

32. Which of the following is NOT a fact stated in the passage?
  A) Many infections occur because people get pathogens on their hands and then touch their own eyes, mouths, or noses.
  B) Antibacterial soaps and warm water are the best way to remove pathogens from hands.
  C) Most hand sanitizers have a concentration of at least 60 percent alcohol.
  D) Hand sanitizer can be an acceptable alternative to hand washing when soap and water aren't available.

33. What is the best summary of this passage?
  A) Many diseases are spread by pathogens that can live on the hands. Hand washing is the best way to remove these pathogens and prevent disease.
  B) Simple hand washing can prevent the spread of many common illnesses, including the flu, the common cold, diarrhea, and many acute respiratory illnesses. Hand sanitizer can also kill the pathogens that cause these diseases.
  C) Simple hand washing with soap and cold water is an effective way to reduce the spread of disease. Antibacterial soaps and hand sanitizers may also be used but are not significantly more effective.
  D) Using hand sanitizer will kill many pathogens but will not remove organic matter. Hand washing with soap and water is a better option when available.

34. Knowing that the temperature of the water does not affect the efficacy of hand washing, one can conclude that water plays an important role in hand washing because it
  A) has antibacterial properties.
  B) physically removes pathogens from hands.
  C) cools hands to make them inhospitable to dangerous bacteria.
  D) is hot enough to kill bacteria.

35. What is the author's primary purpose in writing this essay?
  A) to persuade readers of the importance and effectiveness of hand washing with soap and cold water
  B) to dissuade readers from using hand sanitizer
  C) to explain how many common diseases are spread through daily interaction
  D) to describe the many ways hand washing and hand sanitizer provide health benefits

36. What can the reader conclude from the passage above?

- **A)** Hand washing would do little to limit infections that spread through particles in the air.
- **B)** Hand washing is not necessary for people who do not touch their eyes, mouths, or noses with their hands.
- **C)** Hand sanitizer serves no purpose and should not be used as an alternative to hand washing.
- **D)** Hand sanitizer will likely soon replace hand washing as the preferred method of removing pathogens from hands.

Answer Key

1. **C)** The passage explains that the texture of the grind should not be too large, or the coffee will be weak.

2. **D)** As it is used in the passage, *steep* means to soak in water to extract flavor.

3. **A)** This answer choice explains that if the wrong type of water is chosen, it can negatively impact the flavor of the coffee.

4. **D)** Words like "fresher," "harsher," and "most important" are all subjective and are therefore opinion.

5. **B)** The passage explains how to make a quality cup of coffee by describing several steps with precise details.

6. **B)** The process of the body releasing viruses that have been successfully reproducing during the infection is called viral shedding.

7. **C)** The topic sentence explains that the flu has historically been one of the most common human infections, and the rest of the passage explains why that is, even though it is relatively difficult to contract.

8. **B)** Because these aerosol particles result from coughing or sneezing, *expelled* means ejected, or forced out.

9. **A)** Many infected with the flu unknowingly infect others because their symptoms are undetected for at least twenty-four hours.

10. **C)** The passage explains in the first paragraph that the flu is very deadly and has killed tens of millions in the past 150 years.

11. **C)** Both organisms are harmed in synnecrosis.

12. **C)** Commensalism is a symbiotic relationship where one organism benefits and the other is unaffected. This is the only relationship in which one organism is believed to be unaffected.

13. **A)** The text identifies pollination as mutualistic, so both organisms benefit.

14. **D)** The entire passage is about the different types of symbiotic relationships.

15. **A)** Mutualism is a relationship where both organisms benefit. In this situation, algae and the spider crab are both benefitting from this relationship.

16. **C)** The passage explains that scientists believe that if they can restore the grassland, they will be able to slow climate change by slowing the thawing of the permafrost that lies beneath the tundra.

17. **B)** Scientists believe that the forests are detrimental to the re-creation of the subarctic steppe grassland, and wildlife can knock down trees like they did during the last Ice Age.

18. **C)** This passage is about the subarctic steppe grassland ecosystem that flourished during the last Ice Age.

19. **D)** The passage says that scientists believe the forested terrain was not a natural development, which means humans must have planted the trees.

20. **A)** Scientists hope to bring back the wildlife in this region, especially the wooly mammoth, to help with the clearing of trees.

21. **C)** The value of this spacecraft is that it was able to bring new information to the scientists about Saturn. The unique end to its mission allowed scientists to understand the planet in a way they had not before.

22. **B)** The paragraph detailed the intention of a spacecraft called *Cassini* by explaining its purpose for exploring and the impact its mission had on the study of Saturn.

23. **D)** The passage says that Titan is Saturn's largest moon, which implies that Saturn has more than one moon.

24. **B)** The passage explains that *Cassini* reached the unexplored region between Saturn itself and its famous rings, so little was known at the time about that area.

25. **C)** The passage explains that the spacecraft was designed not to return but to end its journey by diving into Saturn's atmosphere.

26. **B)** The passage explains that Gatling believed fewer soldiers would be needed with the use of the Gatling gun and that it was also a forerunner to the modern machine gun; therefore, we can assume that the gun fired more shots than other guns were able to.

27. **B)** The passage explains that the shaft rotated after the soldier turned a crank.

28. **C)** The passage explains that each Gatling gun was purchased directly by individual commanders, and these weapons were not purchased by the US Army until 1866, after the Civil War.

29. **A)** By creating a gun that shot more bullets at a time, Gatling believed this would reduce the number of soldiers needed, which would in turn reduce the number of casualties of war.

30. **D)** The passage is concerned with the Gatling gun, why it was created, and when it was first used.

31. **D)** The author writes that "hands 'cleaned' with hand sanitizer may still harbor pathogens" because sanitizer "does nothing to remove organic matter" from the hands. The bacteria are not completely washed off, and therefore some are able to continue living on the surface of the hands.

32. B) In the second paragraph, the author writes that the hand washing "process doesn't even require warm water—studies have shown that cold water is just as effective at reducing the number of microbes on the hands. Antibacterial soaps are also available, although several studies have shown that simple soap and cold water is just as effective."

33. C) Together, these sentences provide an adequate summary of the passage overall.

34. B) The author writes that because hand sanitizer "isn't rinsed from hands [as is water], it only kills pathogens and does nothing to remove organic matter."

35. A) Each paragraph examines hand washing from a different angle.

36. A) In the first paragraph, the author writes, "Many illnesses are spread when people touch infected surfaces, such as door handles or other people's hands, and then touch their own eyes, mouths, or noses." The reader can infer from this sentence that hand washing prevents the spread of surface-borne illnesses.

Mathematical Achievement

1. Ken has taken 6 tests in his English class. Each test is worth 100 points. Ken has a 92% average in English. If Ken's first 5 grades are 90, 100, 95, 83, and 87, what was Ken's score on the 6th test?
   - A) 80
   - B) 92
   - C) 97
   - D) 100

2. Simplify: $(1.2 \times 10^{-3})(1.13 \times 10^{-4})$
   - A) 1.356×10^{-7}
   - B) 1.356×10^{-1}
   - C) 1.356×10
   - D) 1.356×10^{12}

3. In a theater, there are 4500 lower-level seats and 2000 upper-level seats. What is the ratio of lower-level seats to total seats?
   - A) $\frac{4}{13}$
   - B) $\frac{4}{9}$
   - C) $\frac{9}{13}$
   - D) $\frac{9}{4}$

4. The population of a town was 7250 in 2014 and 7375 in 2015. What was the percent increase from 2014 to 2015 to the nearest tenth of a percent?
   - A) 1.5%
   - B) 1.6%
   - C) 1.7%
   - D) 1.8%

5. In the fall, 425 students pass the math benchmark. In the spring, 680 students pass the same benchmark. What is the percentage increase in passing scores from fall to spring?
   - A) 37.5%
   - B) 55%
   - C) 60%
   - D) 62.5%

6. A fruit stand sells apples, bananas, and oranges at a ratio of 3:2:1. If the fruit stand sells 20 bananas, how many total pieces of fruit does the fruit stand sell?
   - A) 10
   - B) 30
   - C) 40
   - D) 60

7. Five numbers have an average of 16. If the first 4 numbers have a sum of 68, what is the 5th number?
   - A) 12
   - B) 16
   - C) 52
   - D) 80

8. Multiply: $(5+ \sqrt{5})(5- \sqrt{5})$
   - A) $10\sqrt{5}$
   - B) 20
   - C) 25
   - D) $25\sqrt{5}$

9. Which of the following is the y-intercept of the given equation?
   $7y - 42x + 7 = 0$
   - A) $(-1, 0)$
   - B) $(0, -1)$
   - C) $(0, \frac{1}{6})$
   - D) $(6, 0)$

10. If the average person drinks ten 8-ounce glasses of water each day, how many ounces of water will they drink in a week?

    A) 70 oz
    B) 80 oz
    C) 560 oz
    D) 700 oz

11. Yvonne ran 4.6 miles, 4.8 miles, 5.3 miles, 5.2 miles, and 6 miles on five consecutive days. What was her average distance over the five days?

    A) 4.1 mi
    B) 4.975 mi
    C) 5.18 mi
    D) 25.9 mi

12. Robbie has a bag of treats that contains 5 pieces of gum, 7 pieces of taffy, and 8 pieces of chocolate. If Robbie reaches into the bag and randomly pulls out a treat, what is the probability that he will get a piece of taffy?

    A) $\frac{1}{7}$
    B) $\frac{7}{20}$
    C) $\frac{5}{8}$
    D) 1

13. Micah invites 23 friends to his house and is having pizza for dinner. Each pizza feeds approximately 4 people. Micah wants the least amount left over as possible. How many pizzas should he order?

    A) 4
    B) 5
    C) 6
    D) 7

14. What is the perimeter of the shape?

    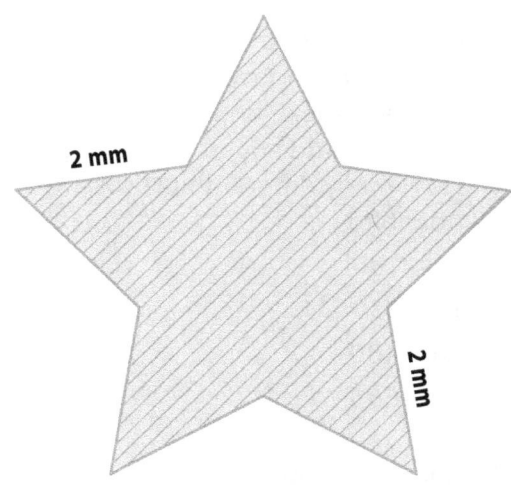

    A) 2 mm
    B) 4 mm
    C) 10 mm
    D) 20 mm

15. A semicircle is drawn next to the base of an isosceles triangle such that its diameter is perpendicular to the triangle's altitude. What is the area of the resulting figure shown below?

    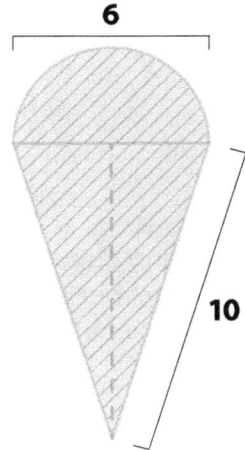

    A) $30 + 4.5\pi$
    B) $30 + 9\pi$
    C) $30 + 36\pi$
    D) $60 + 4.5\pi$

16. A restaurant offers burritos on a corn or a flour tortilla, 5 types of meat, 6 types of cheese, and 3 different salsas. When ordering, customers choose 1 type of tortilla, 1 meat, and 1 cheese. They can add any of the 3 salsas. How many different burritos are possible?
    A) 180
    B) 330
    C) 480
    D) 660

17. Adam is painting the outside of a 4-walled shed. The shed is 5 feet wide, 4 feet deep, and 7 feet high. How many square feet of paint will Adam need to paint the 4 sides of the shed?
    A) 126
    B) 140
    C) 252
    D) 560

18. A 10 L container will hold how much more liquid than a 2-gallon container? (1 gal = 3.785 L)
    A) 2.00 L
    B) 2.43 L
    C) 6.22 L
    D) 8.00 L

19. A cyclist is moving down the sidewalk at 15 feet per second. What is his approximate speed in miles per hour?
    A) 10.2 mph
    B) 15.9 mph
    C) 17.1 mph
    D) 22 mph

20. Matt and Kendall are participating in a raffle in which one ticket will be drawn to find the winner. Matt bought 35 tickets and Kendall bought 15 tickets. If 1250 total tickets were purchased, what is the probability that either Matt or Kendall will win the raffle?
    A) 0.02
    B) 0.03
    C) 0.04
    D) 0.08

21. What number is in the hundredths place when 21.563 is divided by 8?
    A) 5
    B) 6
    C) 8
    D) 9

22. If the circumference of a circle is 18π, what is the area of the circle?
    A) 9π
    B) 18π
    C) 27π
    D) 81π

23. What is the area of the shape below?

    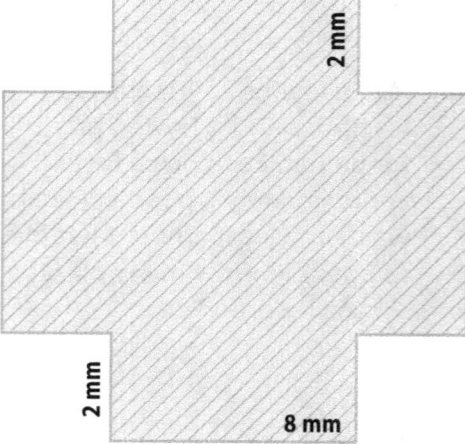

    A) 6 mm²
    B) 16 mm²
    C) 64 mm²

D) 128 mm²

24. Solve: $(50 - 12 \times 4)^2$
    A) 2
    B) 4
    C) 152
    D) 304

25. What is the probability a coin flipped 4 times in a row will be heads all 4 times?
    A) $\frac{1}{32}$
    B) $\frac{1}{16}$
    C) $\frac{1}{8}$
    D) $\frac{1}{4}$

26. Interstate 10 runs 878 miles through Texas, spanning from El Paso to Orange. Paul is expected to deliver items from Orange to El Paso, and they must be in El Paso by 7:00 p.m. If the average speed limit on I-10 is 75 miles per hour, and Paul allows 1 extra hour of travel time for breaks, lunch, and traffic, what is the latest he must leave Orange to be in El Paso to the nearest hour?
    A) 5:00 a.m.
    B) 6:00 a.m.
    C) 7:00 a.m.
    D) 8:00 a.m.

27. A television station in City A reaches 140,000 people, and a television station in City B reaches 250,000 people. Their signals overlap in a region that includes 4% of the people in City A and 2% in City B. How many people can receive both stations?
    A) 10,600
    B) 12,800
    C) 15,000
    D) 23,400

28. Mr. Langston took out a $50,000 loan to start a new video company. He produces a video game that costs $40 to make and sells it for $60. How many copies of the game must he sell to pay off his loan?
    A) 500
    B) 833
    C) 2500
    D) 100,000

29. In baseball, a player's batting average is calculated using the formula average = $\frac{hits}{at\ bats}$. If Forrest has a batting average of .250 and goes to bat 4 times, how many times should he be expected to get a hit?
    A) 1
    B) 3
    C) 4
    D) 16

30. Simplify: $4(a^2 + 2a) - 3(a + 7)$
    A) $4a^2 + 5a - 21$
    B) $4a^2 + 11a - 21$
    C) $4a^2 + 5a + 21$
    D) $9a^2 + 21$

31. A store is going out of business and plans a liquidation sale. The owner decides to mark down items by 20% of their previous price each week. If the store is selling a computer priced at $1000, after how many weeks will the computer be less than half the original price?
    A) 2 weeks
    B) 3 weeks
    C) 4 weeks
    D) 5 weeks

32. Mary earns a weekly base salary of $100 plus 10% commission on items she sells. If her biweekly (two week) paycheck is valued at $520, what is the average value of the items she sold each week?

- **A)** $6400
- **B)** $5200
- **C)** $3200
- **D)** $1600

33. Derek deposits $200 in a bank account that earns a simple interest of 6% each year. Using the formula $A = P(1 + rt)$, about how many years will it take for his account to earn $300 assuming he makes no deposits or withdrawals?

- **A)** 7 years
- **B)** 9 years
- **C)** 17 years
- **D)** 25 years

34. The weather forecast calls for an 80% chance of rain for the next two days. What is the probability it will not rain for the next two days?

- **A)** 4%
- **B)** 10%
- **C)** 20%
- **D)** 64%

35. A room is covered in tiles measuring 3 inches by 3 inches. If the size of the room is 190 square feet, how many tiles must be purchased to cover the room?

- **A)** 21
- **B)** 253
- **C)** 3040
- **D)** 9120

36. A new video game sells for $50. After a few weeks, it gets a 10% discount. All sales have a 10% sales tax added. How much will the game cost after the discount and sales tax are applied?

- **A)** $55
- **B)** $50
- **C)** $49.50
- **D)** $45

37. Demarius is enrolled in a class where 10% of his course average is participation, 40% of his average is quizzes, and 50% of his average is tests. His participation average is a 90 and his quiz average is 85. If the lowest A is a 90, what is the lowest test average he can have to get an A in the class?

- **A)** 47
- **B)** 88
- **C)** 92
- **D)** 94

38. Evaluate the following expression for $r = 315$ and $t = -2$:

$$\frac{r}{5} - 10t$$

- **A)** 43
- **B)** 59
- **C)** 64
- **D)** 83

39. Beth spends $550 per month on rent, which is 25% of her budget. What is Beth's total budget?

- **A)** $1375
- **B)** $1650
- **C)** $2200
- **D)** $2500

40. Dashawn is baking two desserts for Thanksgiving dinner. One recipe calls for $2\frac{1}{2}$ cups of flour, and the other recipe calls for $1\frac{1}{3}$ cups of flour. If the flour canister had 8 cups of flour before he started baking, how much flour is left?

A) $4\frac{1}{6}$ c
B) $4\frac{3}{5}$ c
C) $5\frac{2}{5}$ c
D) $5\frac{5}{6}$ c

41. Sally has $127 in her checking account. An automatic draft takes out $150 for her electric bill. What is her balance after the automatic draft?

A) $23
B) −$23
C) −$123
D) −$277

42. If $\mathbf{B} = \begin{bmatrix} 6 & 4 & 8 \\ -2 & 5 & -3 \end{bmatrix}$ and $\mathbf{C} \begin{bmatrix} -2 & 5 & 7 \\ 1 & -4 & 4 \end{bmatrix}$, find $\mathbf{B} - \mathbf{C}$.

A) $\begin{bmatrix} 8 & -1 & 1 \\ -1 & 9 & 1 \end{bmatrix}$
B) $\begin{bmatrix} 4 & -1 & 1 \\ -3 & 1 & -7 \end{bmatrix}$
C) $\begin{bmatrix} 8 & -1 & 1 \\ -3 & 9 & -7 \end{bmatrix}$
D) $\begin{bmatrix} 4 & -1 & 1 \\ -1 & 1 & 1 \end{bmatrix}$

43. Order from least to greatest: $\frac{7}{10}, \frac{3}{5}$, 0.613, 0.65

A) $\frac{3}{5}, \frac{7}{10}$, 0.65, 0.613
B) $\frac{3}{5}$, 0.613, 0.65, $\frac{7}{10}$
C) $\frac{7}{10}$, 0.65, 0.613, $\frac{3}{5}$
D) 0.613, $\frac{7}{10}$, 0.65, $\frac{3}{5}$

44. A grocery store sold 30% of its pears and had 455 pears remaining. How many pears did the grocery store start with?

A) 602
B) 650
C) 692
D) 700

45. A landscaping company charges 5 cents per square foot for fertilizer. How much would they charge to fertilize a 30-foot-by-50-foot lawn?

A) $7.50
B) $15.00
C) $75.00
D) $150.00

46. In the figure below, triangles ABF and CDE are equilateral. If the perimeter of the figure is 60 inches, what is the area of square BCEF in square inches?

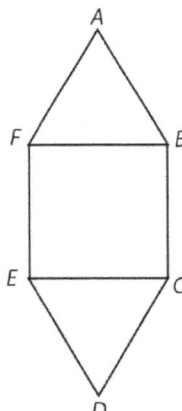

A) 100 in²
B) 120 in²
C) 140 in²
D) 144 in²

47. Points W, X, Y, and Z lie on a circle with center A. If the diameter of the circle is 75, what is the sum of AW, AX, AY, and AZ?

A) 100
B) 125
C) 150
D) 300

Answer Key

1. **C)** Ken has 6 scores that average 92%.

   Total number of points: 92 × 6 = 552.

   Total of first 5 grades: 90 + 100 + 95 + 83 + 87 = 455.

   Subtract to find the score on the 6th test.

   552 − 455 = **97**

2. **A)** Multiply the decimal values.

   1.2 × 1.13 = 1.356

   Add the exponents.

   −3 + (−4) = −7

   $(1.2 \times 10^{-3})(1.13 \times 10^{-4}) = \mathbf{1.356 \times 10^{-7}}$

3. **C)** Total seats = 4500 + 2000 = 6500

   $\frac{\text{lower seats}}{\text{total seats}} = \frac{4500}{6500} = \mathbf{\frac{9}{13}}$

4. **C)** Use the formula for percent change.

   percent change = $\frac{\text{amount of change}}{\text{original amount}}$

   $\frac{7375 - 7250}{7{,}250} \approx 0.017 = \mathbf{1.7\%}$

5. **C)** Use the formula for percent change.

   percent change = $\frac{\text{amount of change}}{\text{original amount}}$

   $\frac{(680 - 425)}{425} \rightarrow \frac{255}{425} \rightarrow 0.60 = \mathbf{60\%}$

6. **D)** Assign variables and write the ratios as fractions. Cross multiply to solve.

   Let x = number of apples

   $\frac{\text{apples}}{\text{bananas}} = \frac{3}{2} = \frac{x}{20}$

   $60x = 2$

   x = 30 apples

   Let y = number of oranges

   $\frac{\text{oranges}}{\text{bananas}} = \frac{1}{2} = \frac{y}{20}$

   $2y = 20$

   y = 10 oranges

   Add the number of apples, oranges, and bananas to find the total.

   30 + 20 + 10 = **60 pieces of fruit**

7. **A)** The average of 5 numbers is 16.

   $\frac{\text{sum}}{5} = 16$

   Solve for the sum.

   16 × 5 = 80

   Subtract to find the 5th number.

   80 − 68 = **12**

8. **B)** Use the FOIL method to multiply binomials.

   $(5 + \sqrt{5})(5 - \sqrt{5})$

   $5(5) - 5(\sqrt{5}) + \sqrt{5}(5) - \sqrt{5}(\sqrt{5})$

   $25 - 5\sqrt{5} + 5\sqrt{5} - 5$

   25 − 5 = **20**

9. **B)** Substitute 0 for x and solve for y.

   $7y - 42x + 7 = 0$

   $7y - 42(0) + 7 = 0$

   $y = -1$

   The y-intercept is at **(0, −1)**.

10. **C)** 1 week = 7 days

    10 × 8 × 7 = **560 oz**

11. **C)** Find the total distance.

    4.6 + 4.8 + 5.3 + 5.2 + 6 = 25.9

    Divide by the number of days.

    25.9 ÷ 5 = **5.18 mi**

12. **B)** $P = \frac{\text{number of favorable outcomes}}{\text{number of possible outcomes}}$

    The total number of possible outcomes is $5 + 7 + 8 = 20$.

    There are 7 pieces of taffy, which is the favorable outcome.

    $P = \frac{\text{number of favorable outcomes}}{\text{number of possible outcomes}} = \frac{7}{20}$

13. **C)** 23 people ÷ 4 people/pizza = 5.75 pizzas. Therefore, he should order **6 pizzas**.

14. **D)** There are 10 sides, and each side is 2 mm in length.

    Add the length of each side to find the total.

    $P = 2(10) =$ **20 mm**

15. **A)** Add the area of the semicircle and the area of the triangle.

    semicircle: $A = \frac{\pi r^2}{2} = \frac{\pi(3)^2}{2} = 4.5\pi$

    triangle: $A = \frac{1}{2}bh = \frac{1}{2}(6)(10) = 30$

    total area = **30 + 4.5π**

16. **C)** Use the fundamental counting principle. Think of the salsa as a yes or no option.

    $(2)(5)(6)(2)(2)(2) =$ **480**

17. **A)** Find the area of all sides of the shed.

    Two walls measure 5 feet by 7 feet. Two walls measure 4 feet by 7 feet.

    $A = 2l_1w_1 + 2l_2w_2$

    $A = 2(5 \text{ ft})(7 \text{ ft}) + 2(4 \text{ ft})(7 \text{ ft})$

    $A = 70 \text{ ft}^2 + 56 \text{ ft}^2 =$ **126 ft²**

18. **B)** Convert gallons to liters.

    $2 \text{ gal} \times \frac{3.785 \text{ L}}{1 \text{ gal}} = 7.57$ L

    Subtract to find the difference in liters.

    10 L − 7.57 L = **2.43 L**

19. **A)** Use dimensional analysis to convert feet to miles and seconds to hours.

    $\frac{15 \text{ ft}}{\text{sec}} \times \frac{3600 \text{ sec}}{1 \text{ hr}} \times \frac{1 \text{ mi}}{5280 \text{ ft}} \approx$ **10.2 mph**

20. **C)** The probability that Matt or Kendall will win is the number of winning tickets (successful outcomes) over the total number of tickets in the raffle (total outcomes).

    $P = \frac{\text{number of favorable outcomes}}{\text{total number of possible outcomes}}$

    $= \frac{35 + 15}{1250} =$ **0.04**

21. **D)** Divide and find the digit in the hundredths place.

    21.563 ÷ 8 = 2.6**9**5375

22. **D)** Use the formula for circumference of the circle to find the radius.

    $C = 2\pi r$

    $18\pi = 2\pi r$

    $r = 9$

    Use the radius to find the area.

    $A = \pi r^2$

    $A = \pi(9)^2$

    $A =$ **81π**

23. **D)** Portion the shape into squares and rectangles. Find the area of each smaller shape.

    Rectangle: $A = l \times w$.

    $A = 8 \times 2 = 16$

    Area of the center square is $A = s^2$.

    $A = 8^2 = 64$

    Add the area of the four rectangles and the center square.

    $4(16) + 64 =$ **128**

24. B) Use order of operations (PEMDAS) to solve the equation.

Parentheses (multiply, then subtract)

$12 \times 4 = 48$

$50 - 48 = 2$

Exponents

$2^2 =$ **4**

25. B) Find the probability of multiple independent events, and multiply the probability of each separate event.

$\frac{1}{2} \times \frac{1}{2} \times \frac{1}{2} \times \frac{1}{2} = \frac{\mathbf{1}}{\mathbf{16}}$

26. B) Find the travel time from Orange to El Paso.

$878 \div 75 = 11.7$ hours

Add the time for breaks.

$11.7 + 1 = 12.7$ hours

Round to the nearest hour: 12.7 hours ≈ 13 hours.

Move counterclockwise; 13 hours before 7:00 p.m. is **6:00 a.m.**

27. A) Determine the number of people in each area that are in the overlap.

City A's area: $140{,}000 \times 0.04 = 5600$

City B's area: $250{,}000 \times 0.02 = 5000$

Total the overlap area.

$5600 + 5000 =$ **10,600**

28. C) Selling price – cost = profit

$60 – $40 = $20

He took out a $50,000 loan. Divide to determine how many copies he must sell.

$50,000 ÷ $20 = **2500 copies**

29. A) Substitute the known values in the formula and solve for the number of hits.

average = $\frac{\text{hits}}{\text{at bats}}$

$0.250 = \frac{\text{hits}}{4}$

hits = **1**

30. A) $4(a^2 + 2a) - 3(a + 7)$

Use the distributive property.

$4a^2 + 8a - 3a - 21$

Combine like terms.

$\mathbf{4a^2 + 5a - 21}$

31. C) Week 1: Mark down the original price by 20%.

$1000(1 - 0.2)$ or $1000(0.8) = \$800$

Week 2: Mark down the previous week's price by another 20%.

$800(0.8) = \$640$

Week 3: Mark down the previous week's price by another 20%.

$640(0.8) = \$512$

Week 4: Mark down the previous week's price by another 20%.

$512(0.8) = \$409.60$

The price of the computer is less than half the original price after **4 weeks**.

32. D) base + commission = paycheck

commission = % × total value of items sold

Let x = the total value of items sold.

The weekly base is $100, but her check is for two weeks, so the base is $200.

$200 + 0.1x = 520$.

$x = \$3200$

Divide by 2 to find the average value since there were 2 weeks.

$\frac{3200}{2} =$ **$1600**

33. **B)** Substitute the values in the formula and solve for *t*.

    A = $300, P = $200, r = 0.06 (6%)

    $A = P(1 + rt)$

    $300 = 200(1 + 0.06t)$

    Divide each side by 200.

    $1.5 = 1 + 0.06t$

    Subtract 1 from both sides.

    $0.5 = 0.06t$

    Divide both sides by 0.06.

    $t = 8.333 \approx$ **9 years**

34. **A)** Each day there is a 80% chance it will rain, there is a 20% chance it will not rain.

    Probability it will not rain = 20% × 20% or 0.2 × 0.2 = 0.04

    Convert to a percent; 0.04 = **4%**.

35. **C)** Convert the size of the room to square inches. (1 foot = 144 square inches)

    190 × 144 = 27,360 square inches

    Area of each tile → 3 in × 3 in = 9 in^2

    Divide the total area by the area of each tile.

    27,360 ÷ 9 = **3040 tiles**

36. **C)** Convert 10% to a decimal and find the discount.

    50 × 0.1 = $5

    Original price − discount = discounted price

    $50 − $5 = $45

    Convert the tax percent to a decimal and calculate the sales tax.

    $45 × 0.1 = $4.50

    Add the sales tax to the discounted price.

    $45 + $4.50 = **$49.50**

37. **D)** Look at the weighted average.

    10% is participation and his grade is a 90.

    0.1(90) = 9

    40% is quiz average and his quiz average is 85.

    0.4(85) = 34

    Write an equation for the total average. Let the test average = *x*.

    $9 + 34 + 0.5x = 90$

    $x = $ **94**

38. **D)** Substitute the given values and simplify.

    $\frac{r}{5} - 10t$

    $r = 315$ and $t = -2$

    $\frac{315}{5} - 10(-2) = 63 + 20 = $ **83**

39. **C)** Use the percent proportion and solve for the whole.

    $\frac{\text{part}}{\text{percent}} = \text{whole}$

    $\frac{550}{0.25} = $ **2200**

40. **A)** Find the total amount of flour used.

    $2\frac{1}{2} + 1\frac{1}{3} = 2\frac{3}{6} + 1\frac{2}{6} = 3\frac{5}{6}$

    Subtract the total used from 8 cups to find the remaining amount.

    $8 - 3\frac{5}{6} = \frac{48}{6} - \frac{23}{6} = \frac{25}{6} = \mathbf{4\frac{1}{6}}$

41. **B)** Subtract to find the new balance.

    $127 + (-150) = $ **−23**

42. **C)** Subtract the corresponding parts of each matrix.

    $\begin{bmatrix} 6 & 4 & 8 \\ -2 & 5 & -3 \end{bmatrix} - \begin{bmatrix} -2 & 5 & 7 \\ 1 & -4 & 4 \end{bmatrix}$

    $= \begin{bmatrix} 6-(-2) & 4-5 & 8-7 \\ -2-1 & 5-(-4) & -3-4 \end{bmatrix}$

    $= \begin{bmatrix} \mathbf{8} & \mathbf{-1} & \mathbf{1} \\ \mathbf{-3} & \mathbf{9} & \mathbf{-7} \end{bmatrix}$

43. **B)** Convert the fractions to decimals.

    $\frac{7}{10} = 0.7$

    $\frac{3}{5} = 0.6$

    Order from least to greatest.

    $0.6 < 0.613 < 0.65 < 0.7$

    Write the values in their original form.

    $\frac{3}{5}$, **0.613, 0.65,** $\frac{7}{10}$

44. **B)** Let p = the original number of pears.

    Convert 30% to a decimal.

    $30\% = 0.3$

    The store has sold $0.30p$ pears.

    Write an equation for the original number minus the number sold equal to 455.

    $p - 0.30p = 455$

    $p = \frac{455}{0.7} =$ **650 pears**

45. **C)** Find the area of the lawn.

    50 feet × 30 feet = 1500 square feet

    Multiply the total number of square feet by the charge per square foot.

    $1500 \times 0.05 =$ **$75.00**

46. **A)** Sides of an equilateral triangle are all the same length. Sides of a square are all the same length. The triangles and the square share a side, so all the lines in the figure are the same length.

    Use the perimeter to find the length of one side.

    60 inches ÷ 6 = 10 inches

    Use the formula for area of a square; $A = s^2$.

    10 in × 10 in = **100 in²**

47. **C)** All the points lie on the circle, so each line segment is a radius.

    radius = $\frac{diameter}{2} = \frac{75}{2} = 37.5$

    The sum of the 4 lines is 4 times the radius.

    $4r = 4(37.5) =$ **150**

ISEE Essay

PROMPT

Topic: School Uniforms: For or Against?

Prompt: Some school districts require uniforms for all students. Teachers and students think this makes it easier to get ready in the morning. Students who cannot afford the latest fashions don't worry if they aren't wearing expensive clothes. But some students feel like they cannot express their personalities or be creative if they must wear certain clothes to school. Write an essay where you express your opinion using examples.

Sample Response

For high school students, every day is a rush of classes, friends, clubs, and homework. Students have so many things to keep track of, so school uniforms make students' lives easier. Some students worry that uniforms will stifle their creativity, but many students unfortunately face bullying over their appearance. Uniforms will take away the bullies' power because everyone will have the same clothes. Having school uniforms means clothes are one less thing to worry about during a busy day. Schools should require school uniforms to reduce bullying and make students' lives easier.

School uniforms prevent students from judging one another by their clothing. Everyone can be friends with everyone else, regardless of how much money their family makes or what trends are popular in fashion and sports. Without clothing to make divisions between students, they will be free to make friends with anyone they want. Bullying over clothing or fashion is reduced because everyone has the same clothing and style. If a student cannot afford the newest shoes or most popular fashions, it doesn't matter, because he or she wouldn't be able wear those clothes to school anyway.

In addition, students lead stressful lives in general. They have homework, family obligations, sports practice, clubs, art, and theater projects. They might need to be at school as early as seven o'clock or at sports practice even earlier. Who wants to get up before the sun to pick out clothes after staying up late working on an assignment? It is a relief for busy students to just put on the same thing every day. They can go off to school knowing they don't have to worry about what everyone else will say—because everyone is wearing the same thing, too!

Creative students will find ways to express themselves through art, music, writing, or relationships. Clothing is not the only way. It is more important for students to have an equal playing field at school. Uniforms save time and reduce stress. Students and schools should embrace them fully.

CHAPTER SEVEN
Appendix

Root Words, Prefixes, and Suffixes

Common Root Words		
ROOT	MEANING	EXAMPLES
alter	other	alternate, alter ego
ambi	both	ambidextrous
ami, amic	love	amiable
amphi	both ends, all sides	amphibian
anthrop	man, human, humanity	misanthrope, anthropologist
apert	open	aperture
aqua	water	aqueduct, aquarium
aud	to hear	audience
auto	self	autobiography
bell	war	belligerent, bellicose
bene	good	benevolent
bio	life	biology
ced	yield, go	secede, intercede
cent	one hundred	century
chron	time	chronological
circum	around	circumference
contra, counter	against	contradict
crac, crat	rule, ruler	autocrat, bureaucrat
crypt	hidden	cryptogram, cryptic

curr, curs, cours	to run	precursory
dict	to say	dictator, dictation
dyna	power	dynamic
dys	bad, hard, unlucky	dysfunctional
equ	equal, even	equanimity
fac	to make, to do	factory
form	shape	reform, conform
fort	strength	fortitude
fract	to break	fracture
grad, gress	step	progression
gram	thing written	epigram
graph	writing	graphic
hetero	different	heterogeneous
homo	same	homogenous
hypo	below, beneath	hypothermia
iso	identical	isolate
ject	throw	projection
logy	study of	biology
luc	light	elucidate
mal	bad	malevolent
meta, met	behind, between	metacognition, behind the thinking
meter, metr	measure	thermometer
micro	small	microbe
mis, miso	hate	misanthrope
mit	to send	transmit
mono	one	monologue
morph	form, shape	morphology
mort	death	mortal
multi	many	multiple
phil	love	philanthropist
port	carry	transportation

pseudo	false	pseudonym
psycho	soul, spirit	psychic
rupt	to break	disruption
scope	viewing instrument	microscope
scrib, scribe	to write	inscription
sect, sec	to cut	section
sequ, secu	follow	consecutive
soph	wisdom, knowledge	philosophy
spect	to look	spectator
struct	to build	restructure
tele	far off	telephone
terr	earth	terrestrial
therm	heat	thermal
vent, vene	to come	convene
vert	turn	vertigo
voc	voice, call	vocalize, evocative

Common Prefixes		
Prefix	**Meaning**	**Examples**
a, an	without, not	anachronism, anhydrous
ab, abs, a	apart, away from	abscission, abnormal
ad	toward	adhere
agere	act	agent
amphi, ambi	round, both sides	ambivalent
ante	before	antedate, anterior
anti	against	antipathy
archos	leader, first, chief	oligarchy
bene	well, favorable	benevolent, beneficent
bi	two	binary, bivalve
caco	bad	cacophony
circum	around	circumnavigate
corpus	body	corporeal

Appendix 159

credo	belief	credible
demos	people	demographic
di	two, double	dimorphism, diatomic
dia	across, through	dialectic
dis	not, apart	disenfranchise
dynasthai	be able	dynamo, dynasty
ego	I, self	egomaniac, egocentric
epi	upon, over	epigram, epiphyte
ex	out	extraneous, extemporaneous
geo	earth	geocentric, geomancy
ideo	idea	ideology, ideation
in	in	induction, indigenous
in, im	not	inexhaustible, immoral
inter	between	interstellar
lexis	word	lexicography
liber	free, book	liberal
locus	place	locality
macro	large	macrophage
micro	small	micron
mono	one, single	monocle, monovalent
mortis	death	moribund
olig	few	oligarchy
peri	around	peripatetic, perineum
poly	many	polygamy
pre	before	prescient
solus	alone	solitary
subter	under, secret	subterfuge
un	not	unsafe
utilis	useful	utilitarian

Common Suffixes

Suffix	Meaning	Examples
able, ible	able, capable	visible
age	act of, state of, result of	wreckage
al	relating to	gradual
algia	pain	myalgia
an, ian	native of, relating to	riparian
ance, ancy	action, process, state	defiance
ary, ery, ory	relating to, quality, place	aviary
cian	processing a specific skill or art	physician
cule, ling	very small	sapling, animalcule
cy	action, function	normalcy
dom	quality, realm	wisdom
ee	one who receives the action	nominee
en	made of, to make	silken
ence, ency	action, state of, quality	urgency
er, or	one who, that which	professor
escent	in the process of	adolescent, senescence
esis, osis	action, process, condition	genesis, neurosis
et, ette	small one, group	baronet, lorgnette
fic	making, causing	specific
ful	full of	frightful
hood	order, condition, quality	adulthood
ice	condition, state, quality	malice
id, ide	connected with, belonging to	bromide
ile	relating to, suited for, capable of	puerile, juvenile
ine	nature of	feminine
ion, sion, tion	act, result, state of	contagion
ish	origin, nature, resembling	impish
ism	system, manner, condition, characteristic	capitalism
ist	one who, that which	artist, flautist

Appendix

ite	nature of, quality of, mineral product	graphite
ity, ty	state of, quality	captivity
ive	causing, making	exhaustive
ize, ise	make	idolize, bowdlerize
ment	act of, state or, result	containment
nomy	law	autonomy, taxonomy
oid	resembling	asteroid, anthropoid
some	like, apt, tending to	gruesome
strat	cover	strata
tude	state of, condition of	aptitude
um	forms single nouns	spectrum
ure	state of, act, process, rank	rupture, rapture
ward	in the direction of	backward
y	inclined to, tend to	faulty

www.ingramcontent.com/pod-product-compliance
Lightning Source LLC
Chambersburg PA
CBHW080738300426
44114CB00019B/2624